PRAISE FOR

Remember Whose Little Girl You Are

"Preachers' kids live with the church, their parents, and the Almighty watching their every move. Although life in a goldfish bowl may not always be fun, it sure makes for some good stories. In this hilarious and heartwarming memoir of growing up in deep-South parsonages, Ellen Nichols takes us on a rollicking journey filled with laugh-out-loud stories, colorful characters, and unforgettable memories of days gone by. *Remember Whose Little Girl You Are* is the kind of enjoyably nostalgic book you'll be eager to recommend to everyone you know."

—**Cassandra King**, Best-Selling Author of *The Sunday Wife*

"Wow, I am just in awe of this book. It was fascinating and inspiring. Some of these stories I've heard about all my life, but it was neat to have them written up, to absorb all the details. And oh, my goodness, it was so entertaining. I laughed, I cried, I was hooting and hollering. I was touched, I wished it was longer. I didn't want it to end.

"It was so courageous and brave of Ellen Nichols to share so vulnerably the intimate details of her life. It really does a great service for women who have been repressed and oppressed and it's just very inspiring. Ellen Nichols is helping pave the way for others of us who may want to share in the future but are fearful of judgment and all that comes with that, from just putting herself out there like she did."

—**Anne Tyler Harshbarger**, Former Principal Ballerina
with Atlanta Ballet, Houston Ballet. Owner of Blossom Body
Awareness https://www.bloss-om.com/

"Ellen Nichols takes us on an uplifting, eye opening and at times jaw dropping ride through her life during a very turbulent and unsettling time in the American South. *Remember Whose Little Girl You Are* is the mesmerizing first-hand account of a preacher's daughter, part of a loving family, that charted its own path, refusing to adhere to the racist times that surrounded them. It's a fascinating journey filled with love, laughter and yes, even some hi-jinx."

—**Chris Sedens**, News Anchor KNX News 97.1 FM Los Angeles

"I am the Robert in this book which I consider a remarkable piece of writing about a remarkable place. The fact that I feature in it is really flattering. My time living in Alabama is among the happiest times in my long, eventful life and the Nichols family was an important part of that.

—**Robert Howell Griffiths**, Emeritus Professor of History at the University of Grenoble, "les Ruines" St Paul de Varces, 38760 FRANCE

Remember Whose Little Girl You Are

by Ellen Nichols

ISBN 978-1-64663-516-0

Published by

 köehlerbooks™

3705 Shore Drive
Virginia Beach, VA 23455
800-435-4811
www.koehlerbooks.com

REMEMBER WHOSE LITTLE GIRL YOU ARE

Ellen Nichols

VIRGINIA BEACH
CAPE CHARLES

Table of Contents

Preface

JUST AFTER MY MOTHER passed away when I was in my forties, the family gathered in her home. We reminisced with a vengeance as if afraid we might forget something treasured. We always thought of our mother as the keeper of the archives, and now she was gone.

We sat, talking quietly, when my ten-year-old niece turned to me and asked, "Who's going to tell us all those stories about you when you were a little girl?" And then everyone launched into recounting the legends they remembered.

I'm not sure it was very kind to review happenings that may have reflected on a recently deceased person's abilities at parenting, but the stories tumbled forth anyway: my running naked down the street, my eating the sugar coating off my mother's pills, and my tackling the kid who tried to steal my birthday presents, but more about those later.

I was born in 1944, the second of four daughters. Our father was a Methodist preacher and our mother was a preacher's daughter. My three sisters were each the epitome of what a preacher's daughter ought to be: modest, caring, chaste, full of good deeds, discerning, and cautious. It fell to me to uphold the popular image of a daughter of the parsonage: wild, willful, religiously disrespectful, incautious, and a trampler of tradition. And oh, I fell to this role with relish and abandon. Indeed, many a waking hour has been devoted to this responsibility.

One of my methods of accomplishing this was to engage persons of the opposite sex to abet my mission. Obviously, those enlisted to assist were the ones well schooled in wreaking misdeeds of their own. I have always been drawn to that kind of person, like the proverbial moth to the flame. Too great a portion of my life has been devoted to not being seen as a goody two-shoes.

Now, none of my escapades were ever malicious. They never involved time spent devising ways to harm others. But I have had a talent in life for often associating myself with persons of the opposite sex who were not as well-intentioned as I. The counterpoint of this attraction to men doing wrong and my fascination with what they were doing was always the glorified notion that I could help redeem them. And if the "save the world" syndrome wasn't bad enough, I was also incredibly naïve. Deep down inside, I just knew everyone was a good person and had only my best interests at heart.

A friend I've known for some years once observed I was guileless. However, he then pointed out that, though I had no guile, I had a dangerous level of "beguile." He conjectured that this deadly combination of "save the world" naïveté and a propensity for blithely trusting everyone, coupled with a "femme fatale" persona, resulted in a life of teetering on the brink of numerous pitfalls.

It all began in a tiny town, just off what is now I-65 in southern Alabama. Because of my father's line of work, we moved from one town to another seven times during my first twenty-two years, but it always seemed as if we were moving from one town to the same town: same town square, same steeples, same Dairy Queen, same playgrounds, same schools.

The Methodist Church made us nomads. And even though our mother tried to make the best of it, emphasizing that a ready-made community was always waiting for us, we learned to be leery of making best friends because we knew we would have to leave them behind. To this day, no one in my family speaks of having a hometown or a house that truly belonged to us. As "children of the parsonage" we were rootless, just a wandering gang without the tents.

The Church had the best of intentions as it moved our dad up the hierarchy smoothly in spite of his controversial views. But it required always starting over, knowing that even though the "ready-made community" my mother referred to welcomed us with open arms, there was a part of us that felt that people missed those who had occupied the parsonage before us and secretly harbored resentment that we had moved in and taken their places.

Georgiana

THE DISTANT SOUND OF a screen door slamming gave the young man pause, but he went ahead and finished running the bath. It was only when he started looking for the bathee that he recalled the door and went running out into the street, frantically calling, "Ellen, Ellen!"

Meanwhile, a teenager walking a couple of blocks away saw a small hairless dog running toward him. As he looked harder, he saw it was a naked three-year-old child. As it got even closer, he realized it was Reverend Nichols' daughter Ellen. He picked her up and headed for the parsonage, mindful that in 1945 small-town southern Alabama, the sight of a Black boy carrying a naked White girl could be his undoing, but that letting her run across streets could be dangerous for her. Fortunately, the first person he encountered was a frantic Reverend Nichols.

"I knew she wasn't supposed to be runnin' down the street like that, naked as a jaybird."

"You're right about that, Charles. But since this is the second time she's pulled this stunt, she herself obviously doesn't see anything wrong with it. Thanks for bringing her safely home."

The incident could be interpreted as a good example of what the young minister would work toward the rest of his life. The Nichols household was not one of tradition regarding the standard relationship between Blacks and Whites of southern Alabama in the 1940s.

The following is quoted from a letter written by my father, the Reverend J. B. Nichols, and published in *The Birmingham News*, October 22, 1946: ". . . Several days ago the first page of the *Montgomery Advertiser* contained candid admissions of political leaders in two great Southern states, in which they openly confessed that they fully intended to keep the Colored population in their states in a political ghetto. . . . When we try to allocate political privileges on some basis other than rightness, we are tampering with the scales of divine justice. Calamity will fall upon Alabama tomorrow if we today thwart the cosmic drive toward justice and freedom for all citizens who are truly qualified."

If you visit the Civil Rights Memorial on the property of the Southern Poverty Law Center in Montgomery, you won't find the name of John Bransford Nichols inscribed on it, but his life cut a swath across an ignominious time in the history of the southern United States. The 1940s, 1950s, and 1960s, and the lives of his children were irrevocably intertwined with his. He lived to be eighty-eight without an ounce of harm done to his physical body. There were those who attempted harm to his emotional and social side without success. He was unrepenting and unrelenting.

We never questioned the attitudes of our family and we never had cause to be ashamed of them. Such an atmosphere at home contributed to a different kind of upbringing. It made it interesting and rewarding, but it sure didn't make it easy. But in those early days, I didn't know anything about that—I was just running naked down the street.

In addition to that tale of the runaway child, my mother, who was a wonderful raconteur, used to tell another story that has stayed with me all these years and which also involved Blacks and Whites working together. I was just a baby, so I have only the memory of my mother's retelling of it, enhanced by my older sister Judy's recollection. She remembered it vividly, although she was only four years old. We had an old 1936 60 HP Ford. It was a big, black, square box of a car—the pictures of it remind me of a London cab. In 1945, it was a miracle we even had a car, never mind gas to run it, so everyone recalls it fondly.

Mother had me, Judy, and our dog Dixie with her in the car. We were riding through the "downtown" section of Georgiana that is bisected neatly by a very wide stretch of railroad tracks. We'd been to the grocery store, which was a major event considering the assemblage involved and an act of faith considering the wartime food rationing. As we rode across the track, the car just gave up. Mother tried and tried to start it but heard the distant train whistle. Frantically, she gathered up the baby and the four-year-old and scrambled out of the car. But alas, Dixie remained to meet her maker. Mother stood helplessly at the side of the track as the train bore down, whistling furiously. Judy was screaming because Dixie was still in the car, but my mother knew there was no way she could go back. She remembered later that her concern was not that the dog was about to be with God or that the only means of transportation we would likely have for a long time was about to be crushed. Her worry was that her ration of milk was in the car, and she knew that was irreplaceable in those times.

Miraculously, men of both colors appeared from nowhere and pushed the car off the tracks. I went back in recent times and found a little sign on a pole just beside the spot where our car had stalled. It said, "To report stalled vehicle blocking crossing or other emergency CALL 1-800-232-0144 and refer to crossing 351271Y." I wondered if our near miss had prompted some version of that sign to go up those fifty years ago.

Georgiana was a town of unsophisticated quietude, and everyone pulled together.

Prattville

IN 1947, THE BISHOP and district superintendents of the Alabama-West Florida Conference of the Methodist Church convened and, among their many decisions, decided my dad should move to the First Methodist Church in Prattville, not that far up the road from Georgiana.

When we got to Prattville, the first exciting thing that affected our cozy little home was that it became even cozier. Daddy's next youngest brother, Robert, came to visit us while he was in medical school at the University of Alabama. No sooner had he joined us than he expressed his concern about my mother's hair becoming very gray, though she was barely thirty years old. He recommended she take vitamin B pills. She bought some; they were pretty and red. She left them in her purse which she put on the chest right beside my crib. Later, when she came back to the bedroom to get me up from my nap, she found a string of little pills neatly lined up along the top of the chest. She almost didn't recognize them because they were no longer red. I had sucked each one long enough to get the yummy red sugar coating off, then stopped when I hit the yucky vitamin part. Uncle Robert was immediately apprised of my ingenuity and determined I would be just fine, though he may have had to give my mother a tranquilizer.

After he stayed with us for a while, my mother said he had an epiphany about her health. He told her, "Eleanor, you know how, in the beginning, I thought your prematurely graying hair was due to lack of vitamins? I was wrong—it's Ellen."

As I got a bit older, I was able to remember some events for myself, although it's mostly traumatic things I remember from that age—like having surgery on my eye.

When I was about one and a half, I had the first of what would be many brushes with death. That one was the result of a severe allergic reaction to the smallpox vaccine. I had seizures, during which my eyes rolled back in my head. Mother noticed my left eye occasionally turned in, a condition people used to refer to as "lazy eye." Thus began years of visiting Dr. Daniel Hagood, who worked in nearby Montgomery, Alabama. I don't remember my first visit, but he often recounted it to others in my presence, so I came to know it well. He said that when he put me up in the big examination chair, I asked, "Dr. Hagood, are you going to fix my peepers?"

Well, he fixed them all right, but it involved major surgery, during which my eyeball was pulled out of my head and the recalcitrant muscle was shortened. I remember being taken to the operating room and that they put something resembling a mesh vegetable strainer over my face and told me to breathe deeply. When I woke up my eyes were covered, but I recall I was in a ward with other children and their parents. Somebody brought me some bells and taught me the song, "To Ride a Cock Horse."

I wore glasses for many years and always traveled from wherever we were all the way to Montgomery for my eye examination. My left eye was farsighted, and my right eye was nearsighted, which was unusual but no challenge for Dr. Hagood. However, as we discovered the hard way, the optician filling the prescriptions did find it difficult. My mother had the habit of taking me back to the doctor to check that the prescription had been filled correctly, except for one time when she was in a big hurry to get home and didn't check with Dr. Hagood. It was only when I went back for my checkup that he discovered the optician had reversed the lenses. For a year, I had wandered around bumping into things and thinking that what I saw, or didn't see, was the way things were supposed to look.

I was not pleased about the little wire-framed glasses that were an integral part of my waking life, and I devised many ways to "lose" them. One involved putting them in the street and watching in dismay as cars gingerly drove around them. I tried hanging them on tree limbs, burying them, and putting them behind books on shelves, but no luck. Those glinty little things always surfaced somehow.

I went to Dr. Hagood for many years until he passed away. I called his nurse "Nurse Anne Fuzzy Wuzzy," a name I think I stole from an Uncle Wiggily story. And even though they were involved in things that were painful and unpleasant for me, I looked forward to my visits and cared for them both very much.

Another incident I remember clear as a bell also involved riding from Prattville over to Montgomery. That would have been my first conscious awareness of my dad's civil rights leanings, although I probably didn't understand it at the time. I was around four years old. We were lumbering along in the same old, black Ford that survived a near miss on the Georgiana train tracks. In the distance was a contingent of men in white robes and pointy hats. A flag with a cross on it was stuck on a pole beside them. They were stopping cars and handing out pamphlets. We slowed as if to take the handout, but just as we got right beside them, my dad leaned out the window and yelled, "You ought to be flying Hitler's flag" and rode off. The full impact of that event didn't dawn on me until years later, but it was an imprint on my memory, filled with a mixture of puzzlement and pride.

Perhaps this is a good place to say that any term quoted in this book to refer to a person's ethnic origin is drawn strictly from the designations that were swirling around at the time. I wasn't yet old enough to ponder the frame of reference used by one of my aunts when referring to people descended from enslaved ancestors. In my own family, there was seldom any reference to a person's skin color, but if the occasion called for it, we used the politically correct term at the time, "Negro." However, one unenlightened and unabashedly racist aunt categorized Black people thusly: "Colored" meant she thought you were quite passable and at the top of her twisted hierarchy. If she had a bit of respect for you, she called you a "nigrah," but if she thought you were pretty lowdown and good for nothin', she nailed you as a "nigger."

Her husband, my father's brother, once sat with my father watching a televised boxing match between a White man and a Black man. The uncle jumped up at one point and yelled at the White boxer something like, "Get that nigger!" My dad leaped up, went over, and yelled right in his face, "He's not a nigger, and you're not a honky!"

I cannot take any credit for an enlightened upbringing. It was the luck of the draw. No one gets to choose their parents, or what their parents do to influence them, or what they choose to instill in them. It wasn't just my aunt and uncle; my peers used the word "nigger" because that was the word used by the people they looked up to. I'm sure studies would show that this was not linked with the socioeconomic status or level of intelligence of Whites using the term. It was probably more demographic; at least, I can't imagine citizens above the Mason-Dixon Line freely floating words and thoughts around the way people did down South. But knowing that friends, teachers, shopkeepers, *and* relatives were using the term didn't make me feel any better about hearing it.

My Family

THE ONES USING SUCH terms were exceptions in my family. To give you a bit more background about my Southern roots, my paternal grandfather, Grover Cleveland Nichols, began his career in the railroad business at the age of fifteen as a "call boy" for the Cotton Belt Route in Jonesboro, Arkansas. As he became more experienced, he moved along into the rolling stock maintenance and management areas, progressing from machinist to foreman to master mechanic superintendent and ultimately to vice president and general manager of the Alabama, Tennessee & Northern Railroad in York, Alabama. While still in Jonesboro, he married Olta Mae Tyler and they had six children—Tyler, Madeline, John Bransford (J. B.), Robert, James Hugh, and Ralph—who went on to become a professor of electrical engineering, a homemaker, a minister, a doctor, a chemical engineer, and a minister, respectively.

Eventually, the family moved to York, Alabama in Sumter County. They were people of unusual accomplishments, but I just knew them as Mawmaw, Pawpaw, Uncle Tyler, Aunt Madeline, Daddy, Uncle Robert, Uncle Jimmy, and Uncle Pinch.

I once asked my father how he came to be so liberal on the subject of race relations in the Deep South, having grown up in the times he did. He said it wasn't really something someone actively told him but that it just came to him one day when he was sixteen. His family members were big Methodist Churchgoers, a church that was then strictly segregated; he thought his own interpretation of the scriptures and teachings of others that he heard there couldn't be reconciled with what was going on in his community. He knew that the Ku Klux Klan had a loyal following in York. He knew Black children, like the family cook's grandson, Jab, didn't go to the nice school he went to. Nor did they take part in the Methodist services his family so faithfully attended.

I asked him why he became thus enlightened, as did Madeline, Robert, James Hugh, and Ralph, while his oldest brother still hung on to those bigoted beliefs. He said it was because he was able to influence all the siblings that were still at home when he himself had his liberal epiphany but that Tyler had already moved out on his own, married, and, to make his bigotry worse, had his wife's influence working on him.

I don't recall him ever mentioning any discussions at home about the rightness or wrongness of the way Black people were treated by White people, but somehow Grover and Olta Mae raised five out of their six children to be people led by conscience and awareness of what was right or wrong with regard to race and a willingness to act on their convictions of what was right. And J. B. led the way.

In later years, after the Nichols family members had died or moved away, a member of the York community, Dr. F. N. Nixon, became a prominent leader in the civil rights struggles of the 1960s and 1970s and was one of the first Black elected officials in Sumter County.

He played an important role in obtaining food stamps and other federal aid for the low-income Black citizens of his region. He was a Baptist minister, president of the Alabama State Missionary Baptist Convention, and a pastor for many years. My Methodist father never knew him, which is a shame. They would have been soul mates.

Although I grew up in that land of legends, the Deep South, I was a combination of that and the mysterious cold "wasteland" to the north, Canada. My mother was born in Toronto. My northern grandparents were highly educated people by way of Victoria College, University of Toronto, and Harvard University. My nana and grandpa, Ella and William Creighton Graham, had photos of themselves being presented to Queen Elizabeth II, in which Ella wore a magnificent ball gown and Will had on a black tie and tails. But at the same time, they were down-to-earth and highly entertaining raconteurs.

At their compound on Lake Simcoe, my grandfather had a study that hung in the air, cantilevered out over the lake. I would sit there with him, quiet as could be, while he worked away on some scholarly paper. You can still order his book, *Prophets and Israel's Culture,* online, though he wrote it in 1933.

My grandmother always made us grandchildren feel like she had all the time in the world for each of us. She called me a "corker," and once I was old enough to understand what that meant I realized what a compliment it was.

At our Southern home, our dinner table conversation revolved around subjects such as the origin of the word *shibboleth.* We learned that the word meant a custom, principle, or belief that distinguishes a certain class or group of people and that thousands of years before the birth of Christ, the people of Gilead used it to identify their enemies, the Ephraimites, based on their pronunciation of the word.

I distinctly remember my father telling us the legend of the witch of Alexandria, Egypt's capital for a thousand years, bridging the time from late BCE to early CE. Reputedly, the witch roamed the streets with a fiery torch in one hand and a pitcher of water in the other, telling anyone that would listen that she wished she could burn Heaven with the torch and quench Hell with the water so that people would love God for himself.

There was a lot to be learned just listening at that table.

My parents loved education, and our home overflowed with books and magazines. One Christmas I asked Santa for books, nothing but books, and he came through valiantly; waiting under the tree for me that year were *Little Women, Little Men, The Prince and the Pauper, Black Beauty, The Adventures of Tom Sawyer, Adventures of Huckleberry Finn, The Little Shepherd of Kingdom Come,* and others.

And then there were the books every Christmas and birthday from my Canadian aunt, Kay Graham, who reviewed children's books for big Saskatchewan newspapers with exotic names like the *Saskatoon Star Phoenix* and the *Regina Leader-Post.* We were thrilled when she wrote us of a typo in her column's title that had her reviewing for *Small Fry Fart* instead of her usual *Small Fry Fare.* We girls thought of writing a thank-you note to the typesetter.

With such noble role models as my grandparents and my mother and father available to me, I have to wonder at my subsequent history of often taking up with questionable friends, especially those of the opposite sex, in my youth. It all started with Virgil, who lived down the street from us in Prattville. He was my constant companion.

Virgil

DOWN SOUTH IN ALABAMA, houses don't usually have basements but are built up off the ground with a decorative grill around the bottom, often with holes here and there, which were great for cats to crawl into and have their kittens and a great place for little kids to play doctor. Virgil's house had just such holes.

It was on the day I turned four that the story of Virgil should begin.

My trooper of a mother had invited some twenty disorderly toddlers to celebrate the occasion and presumed she had the whole show under control. That is, after she recovered from the discovery that the guest of honor had cut off her bangs minutes before the guests arrived. I had one of those Buster Brown haircuts that adults think is so cute and that comes back to haunt you from old photographs. You know, the one that frames the face with a severe square and for which the wearer has to have terminally straight hair. I took the scissors and made it even more severe. To her credit, Eleanor (my mom) forged ahead, later learning to tell the story without even a trace of that "give me strength" tone to it.

Mother had placed my little red wagon at the edge of the yard, and as the partygoers arrived, they deposited their gifts in it before running off to join the fun. I managed to play "pin the tail on the donkey" and "may I?" with one eye riveted on that cache. So, when my shriek announcing the theft resounded across the yard, Virgil hadn't gotten very far. Mother looked up to see one streak about halfway down the block, pulling the red wagon, followed by another streak yelling at a hysterical pitch. She later said she wished she had that tackle on film. Maybe she could have been the mother of the first woman ever invited to play linebacker for the Crimson Tide.

The wagon was retrieved, gifts intact; I was calmed and Virgil was forgiven. However, my family looked back on that attempted theft as we followed Virgil's later crime rampage and noted, "Gee, I guess that's where it first began."

Back to the holes. Virgil's house was particularly high off the ground and in an advanced state of disrepair. In other words, there were lots of places for us to crawl into and, our being three and four, lots of room to stand up and walk around.

Now, even though he was younger than me, Virgil was definitely more advanced in the ways of the world. One thing that puzzled me for some years was that Virgil was already an uncle when he was born. It took me a long time to figure that one out. Anyway, he knew exactly what he was up to, while I hadn't even discovered there was a difference between boys and girls, except one had short hair and wore pants and the other had long hair and wore skirts. I had always marveled that people could tell whether a cat or dog was a male or a female.

Imagine my surprise when Virgil showed me more. We went under the house ostensibly to look at some new kittens but ended up looking at some things that were much more interesting. As you know, I was not at all averse to taking off my clothes, so Virgil had to use little persuasion. We looked at all our body parts and did a lot of touching with no pretense of "playing doctor." All this time later, I remember exactly what we did and that it was very arousing and exciting.

We had several other adventures that smacked of Virgil's fondness for depravity. One involved a bag of money that my dad kept in the top drawer of his dresser. I told Virgil about it, and he just had to see it. Sure enough, we found it right where I said it was, a brown paper bag full of coins. Virgil was all for taking it and heading for the corner store where they had Pixy Stix and firecrackers. Then we got the idea (actually, it sounds more like something a preacher's daughter would dream up, so it was probably my idea) to go around the neighborhood and give away some of the money to our pals. There was a lot to hand out and we could hit the store after we had made our rounds.

We headed out and had probably dispensed half of the booty when my mom came barreling down the sidewalk after us. Evidently, someone's mother thought it odd that we were acting like junior philanthropists and called my mother to ask if she might know whose money we were blithely handing out. Virgil and I were quite indignant that we had to go along the street with her and ask for the money back. Our plans for being the most popular twosome at Prattville Preschool backfired, humiliating us in the process. It turned out the reason there was a bag of money in my dad's drawer was that he was supposed to safeguard the Sunday church service collection until it could be deposited in the bank.

It was already obvious at that point that I didn't have much sense of the Church and its money. Mother loved to tell the tale of my first day at Sunday school. She decked me out in my Sunday best, complete with a little purse with a dime in it, and dropped me off at the classroom door. When I returned home, I turned the purse upside down, and fifty cents in nickels and dimes rolled out. When she questioned me as to where it came from, I told her someone had passed around this plate of money, so I took some.

Prattville was such a small town that many of the streets were unpaved. Our little white house, though quite elegant, was backed by a large field and had a dirt road running along one side.

One day, big trucks arrived. Men jumped out and started measuring the dirt road. A small crowd gathered. The workmen explained they had been sent to pave this particular street and everybody had better stay well back because this was hot and sticky stuff. They marked off the area with poles and rope. The crowd stayed around as long as it was entertaining, then wandered off to other pursuits. Everybody except Virgil and me, that is.

We were fascinated and poked the tar with sticks and built a little stick house for elves using the tar as mortar. When the men finally left, we were still hanging around along the edge of the road. Then Virgil remembered that he once saw some older kids leave their foot- and handprints in cement. We decided this sounded like a great idea. Fortunately for our tender preschool hides, by the time we thought of this, the tar had cooled somewhat. We got about a foot from the edge when we had an experience that prepared us for future school lessons about prehistoric monsters and why they became extinct. We were stuck fast in the tar, and attempts to extricate ourselves made us fall over and get more stuck. Suddenly we had a greater understanding of that bedtime story about Brer Rabbit and the Tar Baby. And even though the tar had cooled, being tar, it burned our skin. We were weeping and wailing, and then our mothers were weeping and wailing because they had to somehow drag us out without getting stuck themselves. Then the task began of trying to get it out of our hair, clothes, and shoes, and off our skin. No one was happy about that.

To add to the mayhem of their lives, my mother and father invited my uncle Robert, Aunt Rowena, and cousins Sue and Ann to come live with us. Robert was just out of medical school, had completed all his internships and residencies, and was looking for a place to set up practice. My dad knew a Dr. Newton who was looking for a partner and introduced him to Robert. The two of them hit it off, formed a highly successful relationship, set up a clinic together, and ultimately built a hospital that still stands today.

Because it takes a while to get a family settled, the other Nicholses lived with us for over a year—long enough for all the kids to have mumps, chickenpox, measles, rampant impetigo, and numerous raucous disagreements. Yes, mayhem was the word of choice when recalling stories about this era in our lives.

One incident that really stuck with me was the time my mother found my little wire-framed spectacles with the earpieces twirled into tight little coils. Of course, she immediately accosted me as the obvious culprit, but I too was mystified. When I first found them missing, I said nothing and looked nowhere. Hooray! No more glasses. It turned out my cousin, Ann, was the guilty party. She was jealous of the fuss the grown-ups made about my glasses in their attempts to encourage me to like them and keep them on. My mother was so upset that she spanked Ann. I remember being really surprised because I didn't know you could spank someone who wasn't your own child.

Once all those cousins moved out, we were left to our own devices for entertainment. Living in a parsonage often led us to play games that might not have been dreamed up by kids in regular homes. One that I remember fondly was when Judy and I would play Palm Sunday. I especially liked it because, for practical reasons centering around size, I got to be Jesus and Judy had to be the donkey. We managed to rig up palm-like branches and artfully draped towels and marched around triumphantly, nodding at the imaginary crowd gathered to cheer us on—a scene marred only by the donkey saying things to Jesus like, "If you don't quit wiggling, we're never going to get to Jerusalem."

We had a functional artesian well in our backyard that played a part in our Good Samaritan reenactments. I loved drinking from that well. Legend has it that my mom looked out the kitchen window one bitterly cold day and saw me, totally naked, with my head poised under the spout. She came charging out and claims that when she asked me what I was doing, I simply answered, "Getting a drink of water." Maybe I wasn't listening when it came to that part in the story about the Garden of Eden when everybody gets embarrassed about not wearing any clothes.

Our family moved away from Prattville while I was still four. In those days, the Methodist Church moved its ministers every three or four years, but we hadn't been there that long. My dad never said he asked for a transfer, but I always wondered if removing me from Virgil's influence had anything to do with the move. We headed for Greenville, some seventy miles away, but because the aunt, uncle, and cousins who had lived with us for a while stayed on in Prattville, I heard from time to time what Virgil was up to.

His real problems seemed to start when he left high school: petty theft and vandalism before moving on to more serious stuff. The most distressing story I heard was about his crimes against Miss Thelma. She was a lovely elderly lady whom everybody in town knew and cared for. Ever since her husband's passing, she lived all alone in their big old rambling house. One night, Virgil broke in. He raped her and robbed her. Even though he blindfolded her so she never saw him, she recognized his voice. He was arrested and brought to trial.

Here is one of the first of many coincidences of my life that show how events and people can be so intertwined even though most of the time they are miles apart and out of touch. Virgil got off with a very light sentence thanks to the skills of another friend of my youth, a lawyer who later became a judge and who goes by the unlikely name of Kiwi. Virgil did his time and immediately went back to his life of ill-gotten rewards, namely grand theft, only now with a weapon.

The next time I heard of him, he had taken up with a woman with whom he had gone on a crime spree in Nevada, à la Bonnie and Clyde. There were all-points bulletins out on them as a result of a number of armed robberies of gas stations and grocery stores. A state ranger happened upon their car and found them sleeping inside. When Virgil emerged from the car armed with a shotgun, the ranger shot him.

Later, my dad sent me an obituary with a few short lines stating that Virgil was dead. It was only some years after that, at a reunion with Kiwi, that I heard the true story. Virgil recovered from his gunshot wounds and was somehow released without charges for the Nevada caper. Maybe they just wanted him out of their state. Anyway, he returned to Alabama where he remained true to his chosen lifestyle. After yet another round of robberies with a weapon, he ended up in jail again. This time he hanged himself in his cell.

Probably one of the few decent acts he ever committed.

Ted

BEFORE WE MOVE ON from Prattville, I'd like to remove the bad taste of Virgil from your mind by telling you about a person who appeared at my dad's office at First Methodist Church.

Everything about my dad was open-door policy, so when the tap came on the edge of the doorjamb, all he had to do was raise his head to see his secretary coming toward him with a slightly perplexed look on her face.

"Brother Nichols, you have an unusual visitor—a young Colored man. He says his name is Ted and he wants to see you. He doesn't have an appointment but seems anxious to see you right away."

"Well, Miz Anderson, I'm just honing a eulogy for the ceremony of Stanley Williams, and I am happy to be relieved of such a sad task to meet someone who wants to talk with me. Send him in." J. B. rose and went forward to meet his guest.

A tall young man who looked relaxed and expectant came through the door. His physique seemed to be of someone in their late teens, but his face looked wiser, more like early twenties.

"Hello. I'm J. B. Nichols," my dad said as he put his hand forward. After a slight hesitation at such a gesture of possible friendship from a

White man in the 1950s, the young man put his own hand forward to grasp the minister's.

"Good to see you. How can I be of help?" J. B. proffered.

"I'm Ted," the man said. "And I wanted to meet you."

"Well, let's start with what you know about me, and then I'd like to learn about you."

Ted went on to tell my father how he and his own minister at Prattville's AME Zion Church had had many discussions about the White minister's philosophies and reputation as a freethinker and holder of opinions unfettered by racial bigotry. Ted had become intrigued with such an unusual character and summoned the courage to meet him. He even harbored a previously untold wish that perhaps there would be some job that would give him frequent access to such a mind. Perhaps he could be a yard boy for the church or the parsonage. Maybe the church sexton needed an assistant. He longed for an opportunity to hear White rhetoric different from what he encountered in his own daily experiences.

The two found instant camaraderie that eventually grew into a strong friendship. The closest thing my dad had to a son was John Bradley, my second cousin from Toronto. John's father had abandoned the family, and even though John and J. B. (or Nick, as the Canadians called him) only saw each other in the summer, they were close enough to discuss matters both serious (facts of life) and frivolous (best location for bass fishing in Lake Simcoe).

But here was a young man, right in J. B.'s backyard, who yearned for knowledge and guidance as to what to do with his life. My dad's library, which he opened to Ted without hesitation, was a gold mine of authors with names like Niebuhr, Voltaire, Bonhoeffer, and Wesley.

Ted read and questioned but insisted on giving something back; he turned his strength and energy into making the Prattville parsonage and yard a showcase of landscaping and scrupulous housekeeping. Our floors shone beautifully, and our closets and drawers and rooms were immaculate. No more running around screeching, "Who has my white tennis shoes?" or berating some smaller child for scrambling everything into a mishmash. Ted was so meticulous that my mom once found him trying to iron the puckers out of a seersucker shirt.

As I've mentioned before, each summer we made the trek to Roches Point along Lake Simcoe in Ontario, Canada. One summer, my parents decided that we could somehow wedge Ted into the Nash Rambler along with the six of us. He needed to see the world beyond Prattville, Alabama. And see it he did. We children kind of envied that he got to sleep out in the car every night, not realizing until later in life that it was because he wouldn't have been allowed to sleep in the motels our family slept in.

We took the East Coast route, stopping off in Richmond, Virginia to see my aunt, uncle, and cousins there and take in all the sights of Jamestown, Yorktown, and Williamsburg. Then it was on to Mount Vernon, Monticello, and eventually Washington, DC. I recall the photos washed away by Hurricane Ivan (a story for a different time) contained photos of Ted proudly standing at the feet of Abraham Lincoln. The travel route also included several Civil War battlefields and much discussion of how brothers could take up muskets against brothers and ever have their world be a place where they could come together again.

I learned more on that trip to Canada than on all the other summer trips combined. It may have been that Ted's presence caused the four little girls to behave themselves better in a sort of a form of showing off. The usual trips included ferocious arguments over who was going to sit where and measurements requiring calipers to prove that "her leg is stuck over in my place." Those were the days before seat belts and bucket seats, so it was one big wedge fest with everyone vying to either sit by Ted or up front between Mom and Dad. The ride through the Smoky Mountains probably tested my father's good nature. The thought of having someone tumble over one of the numerous overlooks must have been tempting.

But because we were sort of behaving, for once we really listened. George Washington, Lord Cornwallis, Abraham Lincoln, Ulysses S. Grant, Stonewall Jackson, and Thomas Jefferson came alive in our hearts and minds. My parents were both devoted raconteurs who could make history become contemporary in little girls' imaginations.

A couple of years later we moved from Prattville and Ted stayed behind, but he and my dad kept in touch for years and he has lived on in the hearts of the Nichols girls forever.

Greenville

WHEN WE RODE INTO Greenville that first day, Judy and I were plastered to the windows. We saw the school she'd be going to and a downtown that was huge, at least compared to Prattville. Right across the street from our house was a beautiful park, full of clover blossoms. The church was next door to the parsonage and was truly unique among southern churches. It had Norman-style towers instead of a spire and reminded us of the churches in our fairy-tale books.

And the house. The house! We ran from room to room and got lost it was so big. By now, there were three of us little girls, but Marcia was still a baby and so didn't voice a preference. Judy and I ran throughout shrieking, "I want this room" and two seconds later changing our minds, "No, I want that one." The house was so immense we actually ended up with what we called a "junk room." Everybody should have one. You put whatever nobody knows what to do with in there and just keep the door shut. It was a gold mine for games.

And games we played. Those were the carefree years. When you have a baby sister, you don't need the traditional dolls of plaster and cloth. We had our very own "meat doll," and we dressed her up, stuffed her in our doll carriage, and roared around the concrete porch, tipping her over a few times. Mother once found her turning blue in her baby bed. I had tied one of Daddy's ties around her neck, pretending she was a dog, tied the other end to the bed railing, and then run off and left her trying to escape. To this day, Marcia swears that's why she's so pixilated.

Our favorite activity was to "plike" big lady. This was short for "playing like" big lady. We wore Mother's shoes and clothes, and we stuffed oranges in her bras that always fell out at the most inopportune times, wrecking the sophisticated image we hoped for.

We had a next-door neighbor, Carlos Gamble, who also liked to "plike" big lady. Only he was forty years old. He would tell my mother elaborate stories about how he wore gold lamé to some fabulous party. The real delusion, the true "pliking," was not what he believed he wore but that he believed there was any party in 1940s Greenville fancy enough for gold lamé. We little girls were given a hard-and-fast rule that we couldn't step over the line dividing our property from the Gambles. I'm not sure what my mother thought he was going to do to us short of borrowing a few outfits, but she erred on the side of caution.

My most favorite friend in those days was a little boy named Junior whose grandfather was the church custodian. I think their last name was Kendrick. Neither one of us was old enough to go to school yet, so we spent our weekdays together roaming through the Sunday school rooms, climbing trees, and enjoying each other's company. We loved to lie down in front of the church and look up at the towers, which gave the sensation that they were going to fall over on us.

One day we went inside the church where the organist, Mrs. Nall, was practicing. I introduced Junior to her as my best friend. I can still see the look on her face, one I would come to recognize in later years as the look a White girl got whose best friend was Black.

When the time came for me to go to the school I'd seen that first day, I just couldn't understand why Junior couldn't go too. He had to go to a different school, which seemed odd to me because as far as I knew, there was only one school that anybody ever talked about. And he couldn't go to church or Sunday school with me. In fact, he didn't even come to work with his grandfather on Sunday. It's too bad he couldn't too, as I might have behaved a little better.

Everything was fine in church as long as Mother was there. We had pens and pencils to draw on the church bulletins and little toys to amuse us, and we sang when she sang and stood up and sat down when she did. But then she went into the hospital to have our little sister, Madeline. Marcia was left in the nursery and Judy was given the job of minding me in church. That first Sunday on our own we decided to sit right in the first row. My dad had always complained that everybody sat too far back in the sanctuary, so we wanted to set that right.

Well, things got a little boring down in that first row, so I started to sing when nobody else was and talked a little too loudly and a little too animatedly. Judy claims that she tried to get me to behave. Finally, Daddy stopped in the middle of the service and said, "Ellen, sit down and be quiet!" This was good for about three minutes until I decided that I should resume my singing and that it would go even better with marching. With that, I stood up and staged a one-girl military parade up and down that front pew. Finally, he could stand it no longer, came down out of the pulpit, popped me on the behind, and told me not to make another peep. He recalls that, after church, I marched up to him and said, "Daddy, you embarrassed me to death."

I don't know exactly what caused it—perhaps it was the publicly humiliating church escapade, or perhaps she realized she had a seriously disturbed person living in her home—but Judy announced that she was running away from said home the next day. My immediate question upon hearing her plans was, "Could I have Vernon?" He was her favorite doll. She said "Yes," and I started hurrying her out the door. Mother made her a lunch, wrapped up some clothes and a toothbrush in a little bindle, kissed her goodbye, and stood in the doorway, watching as she trundled off down the street. She made it to the corner, then sat down and ate the lunch. I was too busy playing with Vernon to notice her return until she walked in and snatched him right out of my loving hands. That was my first eye-opener that people do not always do what they say they will do. And though I wept and hollered about her promise that I could have Vernon, that was the last time she ever allowed me to come near him.

Eventually, I would go to that school we saw as we were driving into town that first day, but for now, it was kindergarten for me, and I loved it. We played games, sang our hearts out, made collages, finger-painted, built towers out of blocks, and danced. If this was school, bring it on. The playground's slide, swings, and teeter-totter were really glam compared to the equipment on public playgrounds. Noradeen Stabler, the school's owner and head teacher, kept everything painted and polished to perfection.

It was at kindergarten I first developed a sense of the importance of clothes and personal style. All I had to work with were hand-me-downs, but I managed to wheedle a new pair of shoes out of my mother—miniature red penny loafers that she let me wear to bed the first night I had them.

Have I mentioned yet how exceptional my mom was? She was never the type of parent who measured everything so each of us four girls got exactly the same things. Nobody else got any red penny loafers and nobody else got to wear their new shoes to bed. I'm not sure anybody else ever asked, but I just know that if they did, she would have said, "No, that's Ellen's private domain." She was very aware of the importance of promoting individuality, and though she may have cringed a few times over the years, she pampered and pushed our little egos just the right amount to make each of us unique.

With regard to her second-born, I think she recognized the fashionista in the making in me because she taught me how to cut fabric and use the sewing machine. She had made one of the smaller of the many rooms upstairs into a little sewing nook. I remember the first garment I ever fashioned on my own. She gave me two squares of yellow calico and asked me how I could make them into something I could wear. I quickly figured out that if I put the squares together and sewed the top of one corner and the top of the other corner, I could pull it over my head and voila! a blouse. It took me a few drafty moments parading around in it to realize if I sewed down each side, leaving enough open space for my stick arms, that this was a usable article of clothing. I can't remember actually wearing it anywhere, but I'm sure I did.

Later, when we moved to Pensacola, I discovered Van Meter's Store and learned how endearing fabric could be, fabric that filled my twelve-year-old heart with lust. One visit, I was drawn across the store floor by the sight of pink cloth with Mickey and Goofy frolicking all over it. I knew I just had to have it. I made the perfect pair of Bermuda shorts with suspenders, found the perfect T-shirt in matching pink, and then got pink tennis shoes beyond any twelve-year-old's dream. That outfit made me want to dance. And sure enough, the first time I wore it and went prancing down Baylen Street—a moment of carefree spark headed for the park—I was met by two kids who gave me the best compliment I have ever had. They told me they really loved my outfit and said I surely did know how to start a fad: the embodiment of childish style and groove.

But enough about clothes. I was about to revisit that preacher's kid lament—moving! Brewton beckoned, and I had to leave Junior behind, but I found another soul mate when we moved.

Brewton

NESTLED BETWEEN BURNT CORN Creek and Murder Creek, Brewton was a lumber town whose main product was easily transported by railcar and by boats along the afore-mentioned little waterways.

Our house was minute compared to the one we had left behind in Greenville, so Marcia and I doubled up in one bedroom. Madeline was still in the baby crib in Mom and Dad's room, and Judy had her own little room. Strangely enough, there was a beautifully decorated guest room that was frequently uninhabited.

However, if one of us girls was sick and had to stay home from school, Mom let us lie in the big guest bed and look out the huge window as she plied us with soft drinks and medicine. The window looked right across the street to my school, which made it delicious to watch those poor kids go about their normal school day.

On one of these occasions, I awoke to see a largish dog lying in the roadway, not moving an inch. I finally figured out he was dead and started some very serious praying. After all, in the Bible people were always being raised from the dead, so how hard could it be to revive a mere dog? Around midday, a garbage truck arrived and

34

shoveled him into the back and drove off. I think my belief in the power of prayer was seriously curtailed that day.

Now more about the usual bedroom arrangements. Marcia and I managed to sleep each night without coming to blows but only because we made sure Teddy Bear Grover slept between us. God forbid that our own skins should ever touch.

One summer, we found the perfect solution to our forced togetherness; we slept out every night in our backyard. Mother had given me all kinds of jobs to earn money, like polishing silverware that didn't really need polishing and picking up pecans from the yard. I saved up to buy a tent from the Sears, Roebuck and Co. catalog. It was one of those umbrella styles that had little screened windows. Daddy made bouncy wooden platforms to keep our bedding off the ground and we loved it. Until then, Marcia and I and our friends had camped out in our Nash Rambler, which had seats that folded down into a bed. That was fun, but the tent made it a bona fide adventure.

So much of an adventure that Madeline, who was now almost three years old, decided that she wanted to sleep in the tent, too. Every night we made a little pallet for her, and every night, just as Marcia and I were falling asleep, Madeline would start crying and want to go inside. Each night, we had to take her back into the house. We played this game for about a week before we had a serious discussion with our parents, who then used various ploys to keep Madeline inside.

One morning, I woke up in the tent and a small cat was sitting on my chest. I immediately named her Lulu and presumed she had come to live with me, but Mother insisted I make sure the kitten wasn't someone's beloved lost pet. She made me go all around the neighborhood and find out if "Lulu" belonged to anyone. I approached everyone with the same, "Does this ugly, stinky, flea-bitten cat belong to you?" and amazingly no one said, "Yes."

The search was over, and no one claimed Lulu, the first pet of my own choosing, not just a family dog. My very own adorable precious little kitty. I fed her, took her around the neighborhood, and made up impossible adventures as to her beginnings. But alas, I forgot to teach her not to sleep under car tires. Lulu was squashed beyond redemption by a family friend who was visiting and whom I don't think I ever truly forgave. She was buried with full honors under a tree. Mournful visits and prayers were frequent at first, but time relieves the burden of constant grief, and I moved on to other pursuits.

My dad built us a swing and suspended it from a great big oak tree in our backyard. I recall swinging in it and thinking about how wonderful life was, with the exception of Lulu's demise, and that there couldn't be anything truly bad in such a wonderful world. That was before I read *Bambi*. Anyway, I made a promise to myself that I would always remember that day and my time in the swing, and sure enough, every so often it has wiggled its way back into my consciousness. All was right with the world.

What I had no awareness of at that young age was the immense dissociation between my swing and the swinging of young Black men from trees in the Deep South. Abel Meeropol had written the poem "Strange Fruit" in 1938, then set it to music. Billie Holiday eventually made it a permanent part of America's tapestry of songs of injustice, but I knew nothing of that sitting in my comfy swing. I had no inkling of the tragedies that had befallen and were still befalling families of color, but I would learn later.

One day, after a particularly hearty church supper in which huge platters of food were left behind, my mother decided she would take some of the leftovers to Willie McWilliams, the church janitor. She wasn't sure of his exact address but knew his neighborhood. When she arrived, she got out of the car and asked some men sitting on a porch if they could tell her where Willie McWilliams lived. They said they'd never heard of anyone by that name. She expressed her disappointment, explaining who she was and her intention to give the McWilliams family some delicious food from a church supper. "Oh, you must mean Willie J. McWilliams. He lives in that house across the street."

I didn't really understand the story until I was older. The idea of anyone being threatened by somebody who looked like my mother just didn't occur to me.

My parents always said that Brewton had more than its share of problems. Evidently cirrhosis of the liver was the disease of choice. The town boasted more alcoholics per square inch than any other in that part of the South. One of my favorite Brewton stories was when my parents acted as chaperones for the high school dance and one of the other chaperones, who had evidently been drinking his own brand of punch, kept calling my father "Reverend Nipples." We kids thought this was hilarious and referred to ourselves as the "Nipples Sisters" for some time to come. Brewton was a lumber town and we theorized that bizarre behavior must result from breathing so much sawdust.

It was at this parsonage that I finally got my very own room. Granted, it wasn't big enough to keep a cat in, but since Lulu had departed this earth, I had no cat anyway. Daddy had first converted what might have originally been a walk-in closet into a miniature bedroom for Judy, my older sister. There was sort of a foldaway-style cot that passed for the bed. On the wall across from the bed, my dad had built a mirror with drawers underneath and a closet on either side. The Lilliputians would have loved it. Eventually, Judy got bigger and was moved into that unused guest room and I got the room for Lilliputians. There was just enough room for a small girl to walk between the "built-ins" and the bed. At the end of the bed, again with just enough room to walk between, was a piano. I could almost practice for my lessons without even getting out of bed.

That room was my own private radio station. At first, I started out listening to stuff like *Froggy the Gremlin*. I loved Froggy's magic twanger and tried to make my piano sound like it. As I got older, I discovered *The Shadow* and listened to every episode, reveling in the titillation of his mysteries; only he knew. But my favorite thing was having access to music I never heard in church, music like "Jambalaya (On the Bayou)," which I learned all the words to.

I didn't pick a guitar like Hank Williams did, but I did pick out my own version on the piano. I became so adept at playing and belting out those lyrics that neighbors invited me to their parties so I could sing for their guests. I only realized later that they were amused by it. But I didn't care. I was a "ham" then— still am for that matter. Heck, if only they had had *The Voice* back then. At seven years old, maybe I could have become their youngest contestant. Who wouldn't vote for a seven-year-old twanging out a favorite Hank Williams song? Of course, he and I had the same hometown—Georgiana—so I came by those leanings honestly.

But the most fabulous thing in this room was a door that opened into the side yard. Now, this had very enticing possibilities. I was too young to think of sneaking boys into my boudoir, but it did offer at least one occasion of very real sleuthing—something that might have ended up in the *Guinness World Records* or some journal of medicine.

One afternoon I went through my magic door, and there, under the chinaberry tree covering the entire side yard, were hundreds of dead birds, all lying on their backs, little legs pointing stiffly into the air. I gently prodded several but didn't succeed in reviving a single one. I hadn't yet learned the art of CPR, and I'm not sure how one would do that on a bird, anyway. I ran for the garden hose and sprinkled a few drops on several little bodies. Not a quiver or a twitter.

Much as I hated to let anyone else in on this mystery, I decided I would have to call in the grown-up troops. I ran inside to get my mother. Recognizing my genuine distress, she quickly followed me through the "magic" door. She too was mystified. We knelt down, lifted little wings, and felt for tiny heartbeats. It was a typical summery day, humid with melting heat, and we sat on the ground wondering whom we should call—the vet, animal control, or someone from the local bird-watching association?

Just as we got up to run and ask the operator to connect us with the vet's office, one of the birds beside us moved. Then another, then another. At first, they just rolled around, then one managed to stand up. As it struggled to wobbly walk, my mother started to laugh. As she laughed, more birds stood up and started woozily flopping around. Finally, between gasping breaths, she explained that she was pretty sure the birds were drunk. She picked up several of the many chinaberries interspersed among the birds and realized the intense sun had fermented them, resulting in a rip-roaring drunken orgy for some unsuspecting critters. They usually swooped and flew but had just spent several happy hours enjoying something they probably wouldn't even remember.

We eventually escaped the town where many of the residents, including a number of birds, were addicted to the fruit of the vine and the chinaberry tree. But some years later, when I was in college and lived in the nearby town of Andalusia, I was persuaded by my friend, Faye Croft, to go to a dance in Brewton. She was madly in love with James Mormon, whom I recalled from my grammar school days, and he had invited her. So, Faye, my date, and I set out. When we arrived at James's house, he took us back to the recreation room and fixed everybody a drink. It was obvious he had a serious head start on us. The television set was blaring away and yet another boxing match was in progress between a White man and a "Colored man" (still the terminology in the early 1960s). The guys became engrossed in the bout while Faye and I fretted about being late for the dance. Suddenly, James jumped up, ran over, and grabbed a shotgun from a rack on the wall, yelled "I'm gonna get that nigger," and shot the hell out of the TV. His parents, who were in another room, never even came to ask what happened. As I understand, they both died of Brewton's "disease of choice" later in life and so probably didn't notice, much less care. The strangest thing about that evening was that Faye, my date, and I went on ahead to the dance with James as if the three of us hadn't just been in danger of having our heads blown off by a drunken, racist maniac. Brewton was not a place for normal kids to grow up in.

$\mathscr{P}udder$

LATER IN MY LIFE, the newspaper clipping arrived with words penciled across the top in my father's hand: "Could this perchance be Pudder?" The headline was "Prominent Chemist Gets Nine Years."

I only had to read the name "Edward Everage" and "originally from Brewton, Alabama," to know that, yes indeed, this was the "Pudder" of my youth, the love of my grammar school days, the missionary aspirant, the perfect match for the little Methodist preacher's daughter. Memories of rolling in the Johnny jump-ups each spring wafted across my mind. He was over at my house when I had my first encounter with death—when news came that my grandfather had passed. I was seven. My phone number was nine. Back then, life was simple.

Now, some thirty years later, according to a news clipping that had come out of the blue, he was in the county jail accused of murder. What could have gone so wrong in those out-of-touch years? As I read the article, a story unfolded of a marriage gone awry with an unsuitable, inexplicable denouement.

I last saw Pudder at the end of fourth grade when my family moved to Pensacola. My dad was to become the pastor at First Methodist Church there, and even though I was sad to leave Brewton, I felt as if we were moving to a big city, and I was excited. But I knew I would miss my first love. We had as poignant a farewell as one can have at age ten. We had no discussion of when we might see each other again. As we were too young to drive or ride a bus or a train alone, we made no plans. Long-distance phoning never occurred to us. However, we had been betrothed, by junior standards, so it had its moments.

Pudder eventually evolved into Edward, probably because the calligrapher refused to inscribe "Pudder" on the many diplomas that followed. He became a renowned chemist working for Monsanto but was best known for his multifaceted computer skills. Along the way, he married a Northern girl, had two sons, and settled in Pensacola. My dad had also retired near Pensacola and read all the newspapers in the area.

My only knowledge of Pudder's après-moi life was through that same friend who had defended Virgil—Kiwi. (What is it with Southern men and their nicknames?) Kiwi had negotiated a fine settlement for Edward and his wife after they had been in a serious car accident. Kiwi's main recollection of the case was that the wife had weighed no less than 200 pounds and had been very difficult to deal with.

So difficult, in fact, that Edward had found it intolerable to be with her and decided to take his own life, or so he told the jury. And thus, a harmless-looking Contac cold capsule filled with cyanide sat innocently on the medicine cabinet shelf, waiting for Edward to work up the courage to do himself in. You can imagine his consternation when he arrived home one day to discover his wife had accidentally taken the fatal capsule. Now, the "accidentally" might have been pretty believable had she not ended up in a freezer in mini storage.

I couldn't help but remember Kiwi saying his wife weighed over 200 pounds, and Edward weighed approximately half that. Disrespectful as it was, I pondered the difficulties he must have encountered while trying to get her into what the papers described as an upright freezer. The implications made the "accidental" part of the yarn pale even further. But he did manage to get her into the freezer and tie it with a rope to ensure the door didn't flop open. He secured a unit at the local mini storage and hired a moving company to move the freezer to the warehouse where, alas, no one thought to plug it in.

Questions started to fly such as "Where's Mom?" from the kids, "where is Sis?" from the sibling trying to get in touch, and "where is Mrs. Everage?" who forgot to make her promised cake for the school sale. Everyone already suspected the marriage wasn't going too well, so Edward's answer that she had decided to get away to think about things and hadn't told him where she was going sounded believable. However, after a while, the sister became suspicious of his story and began her own investigation. She called in the police, who found nothing, but the stir she created finally attracted attention. Unfortunately for Edward, the freezer mover was a newspaper reader, and everything began to unravel.

At the trial, Edward wept as he told an elaborate story of his suicide plans because of his wife's abusive personality. He had the jury in tears as he described his anguish at discovering the awful mistake and how he held her dying body in his arms. As I was to learn in later years from a high school friend who had been the presiding judge, the whole town's sympathy had been with Edward because of his wife's difficult personality. It was only because they couldn't explain away the freezer that the jury found him guilty at all. But they did ask that the extenuating circumstances be considered in sentencing. The judge had also been caught up in this seemingly meek, mild, milquetoast's tale and handed down the most lenient of sentences possible: nine years with a chance of parole in three.

Now, wouldn't you think this murderer would sit back, thank his lucky stars, and ride out his time behaving well? Oh no, he indignantly decided to appeal.

New hearing, new judge—sensible judge, incensed judge—and new sentence: thirty-two years with no chance of parole until his sons reached the age of twenty-one. This time, more notice was taken of discrepancies in the story. Why would someone of Edward's obvious intelligence leave a lethal Contac cold pill loose in a medicine cabinet? Why did he hold his dying wife in his arms instead of calling an ambulance? Why not call the police and lament the mistake in hopes of a manslaughter charge? After all, he was a pretty good actor, as proved by the first jury's sympathy. But most of all, why the freezer? Why the mini storage? The second judge weighed all this and decided he was a danger to his children as well, hence the requirement that he remain in jail without parole until his sons grew up.

My dad was good about sending me clippings from his local paper in Pensacola, where Pudder/Edward committed the crime and was first incarcerated. This retired Methodist minister seemed to take some vicarious delight in the whole saga and never seemed to wonder, as I did, what might have led up to innocent Pudder turning into the murdering fool Edward. I recalled Pudder's very well-behaved family—paragons of the community, as the saying goes. His parents ran the downtown shoe store for many years before retiring and becoming Baptist missionaries. Was there an unrecognized bully who turned him into a vengeful person? Did some Jezebel break his heart and turn him into a woman-hater? Did working with chemicals all his adult life create some malevolent twist in his brain? Did he just hide his Hyde side all those years?

The newspaper articles reported him staying an inordinate amount of time in the county jail, considering he was a convicted murderer. It seems there was some kind of hold up while he was awaiting his transfer to the state penitentiary. He had kindly devised a software program custom-designed for the county jail's needs and diligently started putting all their criminal records on a computer. The state penitentiary instituted legal proceedings to speed up his transfer. Evidently, they had some computer plans of their own.

I couldn't help wondering why he didn't just get a divorce. Maybe he just wanted her off the face of this earth. Or maybe it was because he was originally from Alabama and murder was such a good ol' Southern Gothic solution.

Pensacola

WE MOVED TO PENSACOLA the summer before I started fifth grade. Boy, if we had thought Brewton was big-time, Pensacola was cosmopolitan beyond our wildest imaginings. The streets had names like Intendencia, La Rua, Cervantes, Aragon, and Seville. Each year, there was the Fiesta of Five Flags that celebrated the five countries that had sovereignty over Pensacola throughout its history: Spain, France, Britain, the Confederacy, and finally the United States of America. The festivities were held for ten days, during the first two weeks in June and were like mini Mardis Gras. Parties and parades abounded.

When we first arrived, we lived in a guest house on the banks of Bayou Texar while the First Methodist parsonage was being renovated. The people who owned the Bayou house lived in a big home on the property and were most generous in making sure the new girls fit in and had a good time. We learned to ride what, back then, was called a jitter board, which was pulled behind a motorboat. They even taught us how to steer the boat. We fished and frolicked and managed to block out how our first visit to what was to be our new home affected us.

Upon arriving at a new parsonage, we always ran from room to room. Only this time we became more and more disgusted. The house's structure was beautiful, but we were dismayed at the sight of wallpaper literally falling off the walls; cracked mirrors; holey screens in windows; dried stuff on walls and floors that we didn't dare ask about; and very weird chairs, tables, dressers, and beds. Most of the furniture had legs of different lengths, which gave you a wonky feeling as if you were walking through one of those lopsided houses that are so much fun at carnivals. But it was creepy when encountered in what was to become one's home. What had the people who lived there before us been doing? For years, Mother prompted us girls toward new levels of housekeeping by reminiscing about the height of the scum in the parsonage bathtub soap dishes, pre-renovation. However, by the time we moved in, it was gorgeous and included brand new soap dishes. Even the furniture had been beautifully restored. Judy and I had a French provincial theme in our bedroom. There were giant mirrors in strategic spots throughout. Skillful workmanship and a lot of care rendered it the most elegant house we had ever seen, never mind lived in.

In Brewton, the six of us had been wedged into a tiny house so tiny I had once decided to move into a closet so I could have a room of my own. I had it fixed up pretty nicely and spent a lot of time in there until Mother found out I was lighting my little dwelling with a candle. That eventually led to my moving into that beloved room with the magic door.

Anyway, the house in Pensacola was huge, though I still had to share a room so we could have a den. At least I had my own, real bed now, not a wobbly cot. And the den had a brand-new couch on which I promptly spilled India ink. My mother turned over the cushion and no one ever mentioned it again. I told you she was a good sport.

This gorgeous house did have one drawback, though. You could walk into our kitchen at night, switch on the light, and try not to be too aghast at the number of roaches you could count before they skittered into the cracks. The highest sighting was thirty, which had nothing to do with the actual number but just how fast you could count before they escaped. And that was in the kitchen amongst all our food. They were so brazen that new ones used to arrive by hanging on the screen door, jumping off as it swung inward.

Fumigators came once a month and sprayed through the whole house, which might explain why none of us four girls ever grew taller than five foot four. To avoid our ingesting remnants of insecticide, not to mention whatever hundreds of little roach feet left behind, everything was sealed in containers. That's why Tupperware was so wildly successful in the South. You might think people just liked to go to those parties, but sanitation and sanity had a lot to do with it.

Also contributing to dulling our senses were the mosquito trucks that roared along the neighborhood streets every couple of weeks in the summer. Most of us never bothered to go indoors when they came along, and some kids even ran along behind hollering at the drivers. I'm sure if it were to be scientifically investigated, a direct correlation would be found between the fumigation of southern towns and the election of politicians such as George Wallace and Lester Maddox.

After arriving in Pensacola, I spent the first two years at P. K. Yonge grammar school being a model student. I loved the library at that school and the librarian, Mrs. Braswell. As had been true for every library I had ever entered thus far in my life, only White children used it. Indeed, only White children went to the school. I mention this because it was in that very library that I had a childhood epiphany

The P. K. Yonge School library had a collection of pumpkin-hued biographies that I devoured. And lo and behold, those orange books included stories about Black people who had accomplished great feats—George Washington Carver, Booker T. Washington, Marian Anderson, Sojourner Truth, James Weldon Johnson, James Baldwin. Already indoctrinated at home as to the evils of segregation, those books just cemented that feeling that we are all equal and we should treat each other that way.

I had another enlightenment while at that same grammar school. For the first time, the stigma of being a P K (preacher's kid) reared its ugly head. My first awareness of this syndrome happened one day when a group of girls and I were over at Elizabeth Harper's house. Everyone headed for her garage and I understandably followed, at which time they all turned and said, "You can't go with us. You're a preacher's daughter." I later found out it was because they were going to tell dirty jokes and felt uncomfortable having "the preacher's daughter" along. I felt mystified, left out, and had a sinking feeling that there was something wrong with me.

Another incident cemented that feeling when I overheard someone use the word "queer" in an odd way and went over and asked what she meant. You've never seen such scrambling and fidgeting as that person tried not to tell me and finally said she couldn't because I was "the preacher's daughter." Throughout my teenage years, my peers seemed to have some notion that being part of the sex education of a child of the parsonage was a one-way ticket to Hell.

This event and others like it were to color many of the activities of my life from then on as I tried to prove I was one of the gang and not a goody-goody who needed to be excluded. My dedication to seeming fearless spilled over into church activities. One summer at Bible school while playing "red rover," I held on to a teacher's hand so tightly that, as the opponent tried to plunge his way through my team's line, the force twirled me around, and I hit the teacher's nose and broke my finger. I don't recall how it affected her nose, but they took me off to the hospital immediately. I sat in the admissions office and read a sign that has stayed with me ever since:

One truth we gain from living through the years:
Fear brings more pain than the pain it fears.

I think they were onto something with that.

My finger ended up in a very weird position, so the decision was made to perform surgery on it. As I succumbed to the anesthesia, I saw a big world with a sign on top of it that read "The End" and a small dot curving its way toward the sign. I don't recall the dot reaching the sign, and I did wake up in what appeared to be a hospital room, not a place with angels or guys in red suits with pointy tails. The nurses told me that when I was still in the OR and starting to come to, someone said, "Hold still so we can take a picture." Evidently, I replied, "I'm trying to smile." Ever the people pleaser.

Footnote: I later read that "red rover" has been banned from school playgrounds. Glad to hear it.

At the age of thirteen, I left grammar school and arrived at A.V. Clubbs Junior High and discovered boys. I was an accident waiting to happen.

My first real boyfriend, the first person I ever romantically kissed, was a boy named John Edwards. I don't know why he was interested in me at that time because I was still in the stick-insect-figure stage of my life. I had thick glasses, braces, and a hairdo that, looking back, I think I must have modeled on Little Lulu's—you know, the two little balls of curls across the front, then straight hair hanging down the sides with balls of curls on the ends? And if you'll recall the aforementioned terminally straight hair, I had to go to considerable trouble to achieve such a look in the first place.

Anyway, for reasons unbeknownst to me to this day, John Edwards liked me. To give you an idea as to why this seemed so unbelievable, I must give you an idea of how incredibly attractive John Edwards was. The biggest clue is that he later changed his name to Michael Edwards and moved to California where he became a model and actor (small part in *Mommie Dearest* and several television commercials). He lived with Priscilla Presley for seven years and wrote a book called, *Priscilla, Elvis and Me*. I briefly toyed with the idea of doing a sequel, *Priscilla, Elvis, Michael (John) and Me*, but I decided basing an entire book on a few kisses on a hayride, some junior high love notes, and the wearing of his ID bracelet was a bit of a stretch. As his relationship with Priscilla progressed, I watched the supermarket headlines faithfully and was rewarded often with photos and stories of him and her in which he always lied about his age. One of the last had as its headline "My Forbidden Love for Presley's 13-Year-Old Daughter, Lisa Marie." Hmmm. I was thirteen when he was enamored of me. Maybe there's a pattern there.

Other beaus followed. There was one I especially liked named Horace Futral, who was instrumental in making me into the alleged good kisser I am today. Another named Jack King was a world champion water skier in his day and could ski on his bare feet, which impressed me immensely. I had a brief fling with Wright Doyle, the son of an admiral, who grew up (the son not the admiral) to become an Episcopal minister and a missionary to China.

My girlfriends and I and our beaus spent much time over at the beach, where we became addicted to the smell and feel of baby oil and iodine on supple skin. That was before anyone knew that roasting yourself like that could shrivel you up, give you age spots before your time, and even kill you.

Suddenly, I was nearing sixteen and being taught to drive by my not-very-patient father. Usually a man not given to screaming at others, under the stress of trying to teach me to let off on the clutch without shaking everyone's teeth out, he became quite agitated and turned into a totally different person from the father I knew.

We both survived the ordeal, and on my sixteenth birthday, he took me to the highway patrol office, and I passed my driving test the first time. Somehow, I wheedled my way into being allowed to take the car and pick up my good friend, Suzanne Laird. We tooled around the various neighborhoods and just happened to end up on the street of David Burmeister, whom I was madly in love with. As we wheeled down his street, I tried to peek into his window but was suddenly jarred by a squeal from Suzanne. When I came to my senses, I discovered I had driven up into the yard of the house across from David's. Suzanne was a good sport and hopped out of the car and helped me try to pat all the squished flowers back into shape, all the while in dread that David was home and would see us and come out to investigate what we were up to. He never appeared.

Around this time, I got my first bonafide job. Pensacola's claim to fame has always been that it's home to the Pensacola Naval Air Station. In those days, anyone in the Navy who aspired to become a pilot had to go to Pensacola for training. This training included learning how to take off from and land on an aircraft carrier. The one in the harbor in those days was the USS *Antietam*. The chaplain of the *Antietam* called my dad to ask if he knew anyone willing and able to come out to the carrier and play the organ for Sunday service. My dad volunteered me, a seemingly reckless decision considering he was sending a sixteen-year-old out to mingle with hundreds of young men and that said sixteen-year-old had only just received her driver's license. I myself was thrilled.

Each Sunday, I dressed to the nines and drove out to the Naval Air Station where I flashed a nifty little laminated pass at the guard at the gate. Upon arrival at the water's edge, I hopped on a launch that took me out to the carrier. I can still remember the sensation of standing at the bow, my hair blowing in the wind and thinking I had to be the most sophisticated sixteen-year-old on the face of this Earth.

Each week at the carrier, a different "spit and polish" young ensign would meet me and escort me up this amazingly long flight of stairs that wound up the side of the ship. When we finally reached the top, I was brought aboard and escorted to the chapel, which was down in the bowels of the ship. The organ was a little pump organ, the kind you had to pedal frantically to force air through the blower. Only some clever soul had connected the rear end of a vacuum cleaner to the air intake and consequently saved me from having to invent the aerobic workout before Jane Fonda. I was free to concentrate my efforts on hitting the right notes while trying to look at all the handsome guys in the congregation without looking as if I were looking.

Once in the middle of the service, the bosun's pipe went off accompanied by the announcement, "Fire in the mess hall! Fire in the mess hall! All hands on deck!"

Everyone, including the chaplain, ran out, leaving me to wonder how close this mess hall was to the chapel. I had always been escorted everywhere and had no idea how to find my way to the surface, so I just stayed where I was, sniffing for smoke and hoping for the best. When the alarm was over and they filed back into the chapel, there were profuse apologies as they realized they had run off and left me.

Such misadventures were forgivable because of the extremely generous salary I was given for doing something any sixteen-year-old girl with a single hormone in her body would have died to do. They paid me $15.00 per Sunday, which back in 1960 was a lot of money. Too bad there were no copy machines then, as I would love to have a copy of my first-ever paycheck, especially since it was made out to me on the account of the United States Navy Recreation Fund. I wonder what the bank tellers thought when I came in to cash my check. The word "Recreation" must have conjured up all kinds of images.

The job had other perks. I bet I could give a pretty good tour of the flight deck of an aircraft carrier. Each week I had a different escort who always asked if I would like a tour of the ship. I invariably said "yes" and hoped they didn't all compare notes. Another invitation I often took advantage of was when they invited me to have "breakfast" in the officer's wardroom. Those guys had steak, eggs, and French fries every Sunday.

But no flyboys for me. I never dated one of my Naval Air Station guides because there were too many scrumptious boys walking down the halls of Pensacola High.

One particular night has stayed with me vividly for years. I was dating a football player named Ecey Hendrix. He was swoon material and went on to be a football star at Auburn University. One steamy summer night, he took me to a party in the backyard of a friend of his who had hung Japanese lanterns from the tree branches. Because of the intense humidity, each lantern had a misty aura wisping around it. Hundreds of swirling fireflies added to the feeling of being in an exotic, tropical location. We drank beer, ate potato chips and sandwiches, and danced to the latest music of Bo Diddley, Otis Redding, and Solomon Burke, getting closer to our dance partners with the downing of each beer. But the true mating dance began when the host turned off the record player, picked up a trumpet, and played "Tenderly" as if he were born in a New Orleans brothel.

And though I'm sure Ecey and I were "lost in a sigh," I can't remember why eventually we parted ways. I suppose it had to do with me losing myself to the thrall of Monkey Manley.

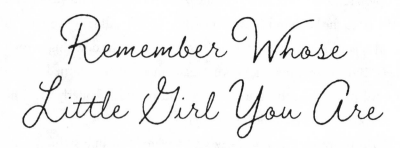

Remember Whose Little Girl You Are

THIS PHRASE WAS ONE well known to the four little Nichols girls. Our mother said it to us whenever we left home, whether we were going to a church function, a peer party, school, or just downtown to meet a friend for a Coke. It is rife with meaning when you're a preacher's daughter.

At first, I thought it was a term of endearment—"remember you are my little girl and that I love you very much." But later, though I still knew it meant she loved me and was happy I was her little girl, I recognized the overtones of "remember you represent your father and me and should set a good example for everyone else."

One time, when I discussed the burden of always having to be good because of my father's profession, her answer was that I should behave well because that was the right thing to do and had nothing to do with my dad's work. In fact, everyone should do the right thing no matter what their parents did for a living.

When I was younger, I spent a lot of time pondering what the right thing to do was until, suddenly, one day I noticed that other people were doing things that looked like they might not be what my parents wanted me to do but seemed to be very enjoyable and not so bad. Maybe my mom and dad weren't as enlightened as they appeared to be.

Monkey

MONKEY'S WAS THE FIRST adult, in-the-flesh penis I had ever seen up close. Previously, I had had several offers but somehow never pulled it off, if you'll pardon the expression.

I had just gone through the "Cinderella" transformation at the beginning of eleventh grade. You know, the one where you get rid of the braces, toss the glasses, get a with-it haircut that doesn't make you look like Little Lulu, discover boys admire your behind and switch from enveloping full skirts to figure-hugging straight skirts, and just generally became aware of the reasons why the big men on campus always asked out the other girls.

Jimmy Manley was just such a big man. He was the ultimate in cool. Even his unusual looks (hence the nickname "Monkey") somehow worked in his favor. He wore immaculate, starched, crisp button-down collar Oxford shirts, chino pants, and Bass Weejuns, and affected an air of knowing everything about everything cool but somehow didn't come across as arrogant. That he would even look at me caused me to feel faint. When he actually asked me for a date, I was speechless and just nodded.

Every boy, with the exception of the aforementioned John, Horace, Jack, and Ecey, who had been enamored with me up until then, had been of the hopelessly academic variety, the ones who grew up to be world-famous heart surgeons, church men, or wildly rich software inventors. So, you can just imagine that when Monkey Manley showed an interest in me, I was smitten.

One of the attractions was that he lived over at the beach. We'd go for long walks, during which he'd make observations such as how the damp breezes were like warm breath on the back of your neck. I think he was the only one in our high school who talked like that, and he seemed wildly bohemian. In hindsight, his parents *were* wildly bohemian. I first saw the famous adult in-the-flesh penis while making out in his beachside bedroom while his parents were supposedly away for the day. It was a bit of an unfortunate sharing of the vision when his mother came crashing into the bedroom and also saw the adult in-the-flesh penis. She seemed much less perturbed about the incident than I. That should have been a clue.

Just when it seemed I had arrived and was moving from the mode of girl-destined-to-make-the-speech-at-graduation (hence of no interest to the cool guys), my father came home one day to announce that we were moving. Not just moving, which was traumatic enough, but moving to a little podunk, hick town back in the state of my birth, lower Alabama. Gawd.

I was uncajolable and inconsolable. I cried until I was dehydrated. But to no avail. Move we must. The Methodist Church had so decreed.

And thus began the ritual of saying goodbye to the Monkey so passionately sought and so briefly in my grasp. We swore eternal devotion and I remember that for some weekends following the fateful departure, either I trekked down to Pensacola, or he trekked up to Andalusia. We wrote. We ran up the phone bill. I cried. I lost weight.

But then school was back in. I entered my senior year at Andalusia High. Monkey went off to college. And lo, there were some pretty cool guys at my new school. Suddenly, I was in the race for homecoming queen, elected "Best Dancer" for the yearbook, and had a plethora of enticing partners to spend my time with. I had a choice of "Rodan," "Snake," "Red Rock," and "King Herod," (those nicknames again) and settled into big-time romance with "Rodan," whom I'll tell you more about later.

And yes, despite the with-it hairdo, the bum-hugging clothes, the straight, brace-less teeth, and the unspectacled eyes, I did make that speech at graduation. Once a nerd, always a nerd. But now at least I was a nerd with a plus.

What happened to the fleetingly beloved Jimmy Manley? Recently, I reconnected with Chip Traynor, a close friend of Jimmy's back in high school who, it would seem, was the last person in our circle to have seen him. Chip told me of the final sighting. Evidently Monkey, who had taken to wearing long, flowing white robes (remember, those were the Haight Ashbury days), had said goodbye to Chip, hopped on a motorcycle, and was never seen again. Shades of Lawrence of Arabia.

Andalusia

MY INCESSANT WEEPING WAS to no avail. My family packed up all our belongings, left Pensacola, and headed north to Andalusia, a little town of maybe 10,000 people. I was still crying but managed to stop for a moment when we pulled up in front of our new house. It was gorgeous. We all piled out and ran from room to room yelling, "Wow, a window seat," "Every room downstairs has nifty glass doors which open out to the back yard," and "Hey, the backyard is huge and there's a train track at the end of it."

It was only after a while of shrieking that we realized there were only three bedrooms. Since there were four of us girls and our two parents, the awful truth started to dawn. We were no better off than we had been in Pensacola where we had to share.

I went back to my crying. Mother pointed out that since my older sister was away at college most of the time, for all intents and purposes, I had a room of my own. We shopped for incredibly prissy peach bedclothes, and my older sister didn't get a vote. God, I loved that room.

As mentioned before, my mother always said when you move into a parsonage and the church it belongs to, you immediately acquire a community of friends. She was right, and even though the weekends of that first Andalusia summer involved much traveling back and forth to Pensacola, I did finally settle in. And lo and behold, the teenagers of Andalusia were fun, interesting, kind-hearted, and best of all, they clasped me to their bosoms. And I clasped back. Pretty soon, all the tragedy of leaving Pensacola wafted away to be replaced by a feeling of belonging to a really decent bunch of kids. No debutante mentality there. Just good ol' down-to-earth folks. That road back to Pensacola, which I had traveled so longingly and expectantly, gradually waned to a wisp of a memory of something that had been pleasant in my past.

I started twelfth grade. Because I was somebody new, I could have been abhorred or adored. Fortunately, my classmates chose the latter option. If you can scrape up a copy of the 1966 Memolusia yearbook, you'll see little Ellen Nichols and her partner Chris Caton under the caption "Best Dancer." Not exactly what my highly educated parents might have hoped for. "Most Likely to Succeed" would have suited them just fine. I did make up for it by giving the salutatory speech at graduation. The first line went, "Buck Rogers has blasted his way from the comic strips into the skies." Those astronauts were working up to that walk on the moon.

It was a miracle I got to make that speech because one teacher in particular would have liked to have seen me *dis*honored. My civics teacher, a Mr. Flowers, took great umbrage when I dared to point out that he was incorrect in saying it was the Negroes who were causing all the trouble during the days of the Freedom Riders. My observation that Martin Luther King's followers had a Gandhi-inspired commitment to non-violent protest fell on deaf ears. I asked, "Aren't you supposed to be teaching us about civil rights in this civics class?"

All hell broke loose. Aided by a truly obnoxious student named Ray Sanders, Mr. Flowers proceeded to tell me I was ignorant and a disgrace to my school. As he did, he turned bright red, and veins throbbed all over his bald head. I was more worried that he would drop dead and I'd be blamed than I was about what my fellow students thought. With the exception of Ray, who acted as if I had the plague, none of the other students seemed to have any problem with my views.

Mr. Flowers got away with a teaching style that I had never encountered before and was never subjected to again in the twenty years I ultimately spent pursuing various levels of education. He projected his own prejudices into his narratives. He laced his revelations about current events, not with a sense of wonder or appreciation that momentous things were happening that caused history to take unforeseen twists and turns, but with his own narrow insights into what he considered were the travails befalling his beloved Alabama. He taught through lips pursed with disapproval as he wove his own negative opinions into whatever he was conveying. I don't recall a single true smile from him, just smirking curves of an unappealing mouth.

My sisters and I had been drinking out of the "Colored" fountains for years and always sat in the back of the bus, so we had learned to take this kind of treatment in stride. Andalusia had a Dairy Queen that had incredibly wonderful foot-long chili dogs, or so we were told. We had trouble getting waited on. The Dairy Queen was strictly take-out and consisted of one huge room, where all the cooking was done, and two windows up front for ordering. Yep, one was for Colored, and one was for White. Same kitchen, same stoves, same cooks, same milkshake machine, same food, same prices, only if you were Colored, they handed it to you out of one window and if you were White, they handed it to you from the other. We never could get waited on because we were at the wrong window. We were always told why we couldn't be waited on, and we were told by White kids, who were the only workers allowed to go up to either window from the inside. We invariably asked what the difference was since, with the exception of the windows, everything else was the same. But we never made any headway.

My first Christmas break included working in the lady's lingerie department at Andalusia's J.C. Penney. A lot of the items were just ordinary underwear but there were a few choice items that would not have been out of place in a Victoria's Secret catalog.

One day, a man approached me for advice. He was grizzled, unkempt, and seemed quite elderly, though perhaps his original youthful looks had just been sapped by time spent wizening in the unyielding sun of the fields. For a farmer he surely was, complete with checkered shirt, well-worn overalls, and a scruffy straw hat. He may have been old, but his spirit wasn't. He knew exactly the type of underthings he wanted to buy. When he called me over, he was standing smack in the "Victoria's Secret" section. What he needed help with was figuring out what size to buy. My first reaction was, "Should I guide him to something more practical, more suitable for a wizened farmer's wife?" Remember, I was just past eighteen and still a neophyte in the relationships between men and women. Fortunately, I didn't offer my opinion because I had a true epiphany as I stood there. What seemed like an unworldly man standing before me was actually a very worldly man. He just wanted to see his hardworking wife decked out like the sex goddess of his dreams.

Now, back to the subject of my life-long dedication to men my parents wouldn't like. You will recall that the major cause of my dehydrated state, brought on by leaving Pensacola, centered around one Monkey Manley. Suddenly, I had new opportunities called Rodan and Snake. See, even the nicknames were up to par.

But before I tell you about them, I will digress to tell you about one of the loves of my life.

Clyde

CLYDE WASN'T A SOUTHERN man. In fact, he wasn't even a man. He was a 1950 Dodge given to our family by a generous church member. My sister Marcia and I immediately confiscated him, drove him around Andalusia in the summer, and took him off to college with us in the fall.

Clyde had a semiautomatic transmission that used something Chrysler called Fluid Drive. You started off in low gear and when you reached a certain speed and lifted your foot off the gas pedal, the car went into the next gear without the driver having to shift. The only catch with Clyde was that his automatic shifting was accompanied by a cacophony of clanking sounds which occasionally caused other car owners to stop and look under their hoods. We would always wave and try to indicate to the other driver that the noises were coming from our car. Fortunately, we weren't shy and tried to drive Clyde with great aplomb.

He was a car for all seasons, although the two front windows wouldn't roll down, causing us to swelter in the summer. As well, whenever it rained, water poured over the dashboard and eventually onto the floor. This didn't matter so much though, as there were many holes in the floor and the water ended up on the ground eventually.

We girls didn't care. We had wheels. And Clyde was so vintage and had such interesting eccentricities that he became sort of a campus mascot, with everyone vying for rides.

I once wrote a paean to Clyde. With apologies to Mr. Kilmer, these are some of the lines:

I think that I shall never see,
A car so dear as Clyde to me.
A car that hasn't any heater,
A car that is a gasoline eater,
A car that toots when changing gears,
A car that bumps and grinds your rears,
A car whose windows won't roll down,
Under whose dashboard you might drown . . .

The only mishap I ever really had with Clyde was one evening when I managed to back him into a ditch from which I could not extract him. A kindly gentleman in a truck stopped and offered to help. He attached one end of a big chain to his truck's bumper and the other end to Clyde's bumper. The result? The man's truck bumper came right off, and Clyde didn't budge. That's when I called Daddy.

This escapade and the many other expenses required to keep Clyde on the road finally led my dad to go to a local gas station and yell, "Anyone want to buy this car for twenty-five dollars? You can take it away if you can get it running." One intrepid mechanic took him up on the deal. We girls, indeed the whole campus, were desolate.

We became even more upset when, several weeks later, my dad received a phone call from the police asking if he owned an old Dodge and recited the license plate number. Daddy told them that yes, he had been the previous owner but had recently sold it. The police told him that the car had been found in a shopping mall parking lot, riddled with bullet holes.

I guess I shouldn't have named him Clyde.

Rodan

MY FIRST GREAT ANDALUSIA enamorment was with Rodan. His sister was in twelfth grade with me, so I had occasion to meet her college-bound brother just before he left to go to Troy State. His real name was Jimmy and he turned me into the heartbreak kid.

"Rodan" was a name that sprang forth because of Jimmy's appearance and his attempts to be Mr. Tough Guy. He was six feet four inches tall and probably weighed well over 200 pounds, but that wasn't big enough for him. He became obsessed with being the next Charles Atlas and lifted weights accordingly. His mishap while bench-pressing 200 pounds added to his Rodan-esque appearance. What had been a normal broken-nose look became a normal severely broken-nose look. The absence of any front teeth, post-accident, made the look even more menacing, though I imagine the original Rodan probably had big, sharp bicuspids.

Well, Jimmy no longer owned bicuspids, so he became my first beau (and as far as I know my only beau to date) with false teeth. Which, of course, he became very adept at flipping in and out when the occasion called for it. Which, strangely, it often did, usually when he wanted to shock someone and especially when someone was being boring and he wanted the person to stop whatever they were doing. I am proud to say he never dropped his bicuspids while we were making out.

We started out with the traditional small-town dates: riding around the Root Beer Stand and stopping while boys and girls rearranged themselves in numerous cars, going to the movies (limited to the one theater and, with any luck, a new show every two weeks), and school-related activities. Football season wasn't bad. Then the exciting stuff began.

Someone's parents had a cottage outside town that, for some reason, always seemed to be empty. The parties were incredible. We listened to Moms Mabley and Redd Foxx and thought we were pretty wicked. The more daring pairs disappeared into various bedrooms. We danced to Ike & Tina Turner and consumed vast quantities of ill-gotten liquor. Because we were all underage, anything stronger than Pepsi had to be obtained from the proprietor of a bootleg business operating out of a tiny wooden shack some miles off the beaten path. There was always the titillation of waiting in the car while the guys went up to the shack and said some password. Nobody ever claimed to have seen the seller, he was just a deep voice out of the gloom. The dreaded police never came.

Interspersed with all this was that age-old pastime: parking. It started out harmlessly enough: kissing, a little groping. Then the heavy stuff started. I was still little Miss Priss preacher's daughter and so presented quite a challenge to Rodan, who felt girls should swoon at his feet while ripping their clothes off apace. Well, it got pretty close, but no cigar. We had some pretty heavy-duty petting rounds, but I maintained my virginity through it all. Activities are a challenge at best when one of your party is six foot four and wedged into a tiny Volkswagen.

Then he went off to pursue his studies at Troy State. My first clue should have been that he never once asked me to visit him there. However, at Christmas, he did seem to make his feelings pretty clear when he gave me a beautiful pearl ring. I don't remember formal talk of marriage, but it was sort of in the air.

One Sunday afternoon some time after Christmas, a friend called and said she'd pick me up for the daytime version of "riding around." The daytime version was for girls only, who did nothing but ride around and talk about boys. After a short time, she drove off the usual route. We ended up in front of Rodan's grandmother's home. A number of cars were gathered in the driveway and on the street. We parked well away from the house, and I presumed I was supposed to guess what was up because the so-called friend just sat there. Finally, I asked what we were doing, and the whole story came out. Rodan was in the process of marrying someone other than the one he had wooed so fervently at Christmas.

On Monday morning, I tromped into the bank where his mother worked and handed her the pearl ring he had given me for Christmas. She looked really embarrassed and mumbled something about how sorry she was. The thing that pissed me off most was that he didn't have the decency to call and tell me. I had to go sit outside the house and be told by someone who wasn't even that good a friend. She probably enjoyed doing it.

Sure enough, several months later I was invited to a baby shower in honor of the impending arrival of the son of Rodan. I went so as not to look like a sore loser and had sweet revenge when the wife turned out to look not unlike the wife of Rodan.

Snake

NOW, FOR SOMETHING COMPLETELY different. Although the same Memolusia that dubbed me "Best Dancer" styled him "Most Unpredictable," Johnny West—aka "Snake"—was truly a guy you could depend on to treat you right.

We dated a bit in high school and during vacations when we were home from college. My favorite memories of him were when he was a counselor at Blue Lake United Methodist Camp near Andalusia. He worked summers as a lifeguard, dishwasher, and general custodian of the Conecuh National Forest. His fellow lifeguards, whom I also knew, were Powers McLeod, Arthur Howington, Rick Wood, and David Alsobrook. They built a retreat and exercise room with weights and benches under the stage of the auditorium at the Camp Dogwood location.

I'm sure there was some serious weight training going on under that stage, but what I recall most is some serious necking that Snake and I did under it. As this was a church camp, the auditorium was used for religious activities, so there was a titillating sense of misadventure when we writhed around "under the stairs" so to speak.

As I did too many times, I didn't give our relationship the consideration and importance that I should have. I was still hung up on the "older" guys. Oh, why do we have the valuable knowledge culled from our experiences at the end of our lives instead of when we're young and really need it? Johnny would have been worth hanging onto because of his kissing abilities alone.

I'm having trouble recalling our escapades accurately because the infamous trysting retreat under the stage was also the hiding place for all the beer and wine the counselors smuggled into that Methodist Camp. The whole experience is tinged with an alcoholic blur. If anyone ever does an archeological dig on the Camp-Dogwood site, they'll be mystified by the number of buried caches of beer cans and wine bottles. I would love to be a fly on the wall when they discuss the significance of their find.

All that imbibing didn't have deleterious effects on those guys' future life accomplishments. David Alsobrook went on to Auburn University and a PhD in history which prepared him for his work with the presidential libraries of James Earl "Jimmy" Carter and George H. W. Bush. He also oversaw the construction, furnishing, and operation of the William J. Clinton Presidential Library and Museum in Little Rock, Arkansas, becoming its director in 2004. No wonder that hideaway under the camp's stage was so beautifully built.

Powers McLeod followed in the footsteps of his father, Powers McLeod Sr., and his grandfather, Fletcher McLeod, and became a Methodist minister via Duke Divinity School. All friends of my father, they fought the good fight to bring Blacks and Whites together in all walks of life, especially with regard to the Methodist Church in the Deep South.

Arthur Howington received a BA from Birmingham-Southern and an MA and PhD in American history from Vanderbilt

University. Last time I checked, he was dean of academic services at Shelton State Community College in Tuscaloosa, Alabama. He's highly regarded for his book *What Sayeth the Law: The Treatment of Slaves and Free Blacks in the State and Local Courts of Tennessee.*

But it is the beloved Snake who was an important part of my late teens and early twenties. We admired each other's minds and bodies (especially) and explored both extensively. Johnny drove an old Dodge Seneca, which we used for the timeless practice of "parking" behind places like the armory on Prestwood Bridge Road in Andalusia. And I have a particularly romantic recollection of a Jon boat ride on a small lake during an evening get together at a friend's. There were also a few more formal affairs held at the country club, where we were dressed for the occasion and behaved ourselves quite properly.

Somehow our relationship transformed from "going steady" into seeing other people. Woe is me for not hanging on to him for dear life. I think I would have avoided many rocky romantic shores while seeking more of the eroticism and pleasure that I had already found in his embrace.

And how did the rest of his life go? He was medical director at the Tampa Bay Oncology Center and served the Tampa area medical community for over thirty years. He has the perfect family: gorgeous wife, accomplished kids, and beautiful grandchildren. Funny, though he was elected "Most Unpredictable" back in high school, he turned out just like I thought he would.

George

NOW ON TO ANOTHER beau who, though totally different from the likes of Virgil, decided to end his life in similar fashion. Sweet, adorable, precious George. What could possibly have happened to him that would cause him to take a gun and blow his own head off? I guess Vietnam happened to him. At least that was everyone's explanation at the time. But, in hindsight, I saw the seeds some years earlier when we courted in Andalusia my senior year in high school

It all started out harmlessly enough. Although I was Methodist, I occasionally played the organ at the little Episcopal church where this family had their membership, a church that struggled to survive in a town where most people were partial to born-again and Full Gospel liturgy.

I knew his family well. They were perfect for the 1960s: successful father, pillar of the community; perfect mother devoted to home, family, and community works; an older daughter who was a cohort of mine from school; and a younger daughter and son who had been faithful visitors to the city playground where I worked in the summer. And then the older brother came home from college for a weekend.

That Sunday, after I wound up the postlude at the church service, his sister proudly introduced me, "Ellen, I'd like you to meet my older brother. This is George." Our eyes met and that was it.

Though he went to Auburn University, some hundreds of miles away, he suddenly seemed to come home more often. And he was such a sweetheart. A handsome young man, not much taller than I, with an impish quality about him. Just perfect for someone like me, whose father had once observed that I always looked for elves in the woods.

We had the usual small town–type dates: seeing whatever was on at the local picture show, riding around the Root Beer Stand to see who else was out riding around the Root Beer Stand, numerous barbeque sandwiches at The Pit, and an innocent kiss or two at the front door until my dad flashed the porch light.

George was a person of varied interests and a lot of fun to be with. My sister recalls he used to blow "Taps" at that same Blue Lake church camp, and always stuck his gum behind his ear just before putting the bugle to his lips.

Looking back, I realize his life was a series of obsessions. When I was involved with him, it was scuba diving, which found him picking me up at 5 a.m. and heading down to Fort Walton Beach to learn. His family had a beautiful cottage and a big powerful boat. We loaded up all the diving gear and our lunch and headed out toward the Gulf.

But it was bad timing. As we rode through a channel past one bit of shore, there was a giant shark beached on the sand. The fact that this particular one was dead made no difference to me. I never left the boat the whole day. I went home with a scraped belly from hanging over the side trying to see what I could with goggles that were never more than six inches under water. But George was such a nice guy. If he minded, he never let on. That's what he was like.

So, I never gave it a second thought when one Sunday night he suggested we go to church. No, that's not true. I did think it was odd because I'd never heard of the Episcopalians having night church. But I thought maybe something special was happening and because I liked their pomp and ritual, I was happy to go.

I soon learned George had grown discontented with that pomp and ritual as we headed to the outskirts of town. There, he led me to a little one-room church called the Holy Gospel & Revival Center (the name alone reeked of small-town fundamentalism). This really wasn't my cup of tea, but I didn't say anything because I liked him. However, at the end of the service I did draw the line at throwing myself on the altar and declaring myself "born again" as everyone else in the congregation did. I was the only one left back in the pews. I was reminded of the time my dear Methodist preacher daddy had taken my sisters and me to see Billy Graham because he thought it was part of history. It was in a Montgomery stadium and Billy held a similar "altar call"—mass salvation on the football field—but I was so removed up in the bleachers it didn't bother me.

This time it did. We were in a sanctuary that was no bigger than thirty-five by twenty feet which was way too close for comfort. George became obsessed with that church and being "born again," and I quickly became unobsessed with him.

I don't recall quite how I extricated myself from that liaison, but I remember being disappointed because I liked him so much. He went on to graduate from Auburn and then left for Vietnam. Oh, the evils of the military draft system, in which no care was taken of the delicate souls who never sought to bear arms. They were shuffled along with everyone else to march to a violent drummer.

A friend later told me George had been wounded and had to lie for several days in a ditch with his dead comrades until help came. He recovered, was discharged, and came back to Alabama, where he married and lived in a trailer. One day, his wife came home to that trailer and found him dead by his own hand, a hand so unfit for holding a gun under any circumstances.

I hope he was right about being born again.

College — Montgomery

THOUGH HIGHLY INTELLIGENT, WELL-EDUCATED
people who were sometimes very liberal in their thinking, my
caring parents were in the thrall of Southern tradition regarding
the aspirations of girls. Betty Friedan hadn't yet enlightened us as
to the pitfalls awaiting girls raised in the 1940s, 1950s, and 1960s
and Germaine Greer was unheard of. We stumbled off with our
parents' blessings to prepare for innocuous "careers" to live lives of
sophisticated good works unblemished by causal reasoning.

There was never any question but that the Nichols girls would all
go to college. This indoctrination was fairly easy because my parents
were both highly educated, and although I don't recall actively talking
about it, we girls always just knew we would go to college.

My father grew up in the small Alabama town of York, where he
seldom wore shoes and never made anything less than an *A* in school.
Neither of his parents were formally educated, but they somehow
instilled a thirst for knowledge in their six children. The boys all went
on to a minimum of seven years each of post-secondary school and

took jobs as doctors, chemical engineers, professors, and ministers. My dad chose the churchly route, starting at Birmingham-Southern where he graduated Phi Beta Kappa and summa cum laude and then went on scholarship to Yale Divinity School. After he graduated from Yale, he won the Two Brothers Fellowship, which sent him to study for a year in Jerusalem at the American School of Oriental Research.

A Canadian named William Creighton Graham, an Old Testament scholar from the University of Chicago doing an exchange professorship in Jerusalem, was my dad's teacher. Fortunately, Dr. Graham had brought his family along, and thus my father met my mother, Eleanor Cook Graham. They fell in love, and once my mother had finished her baccalaureate at the University of Chicago, they married, settling in south Alabama where my dad took up his first charge as a minister at Foley Methodist Church.

So, we four daughters were destined to go to college. In my senior year of high school, I investigated the possibilities according to my parents' wishes and pocketbook, which left Huntingdon College in Montgomery or Birmingham-Southern College in Birmingham. Sending four daughters to college promised to be a great challenge to my parents' financial situation, so we researched all possibilities for monetary help. I gamely went up to Huntingdon College to try out for one of their music scholarships and won one in piano. Never mind that I had no interest in majoring in music. I was also offered a national Methodist scholarship and a United Daughters of the Confederacy stipend, so, all in all, Huntingdon was trying to make it as easy as possible for me to attend.

Then, on another weekend, I trekked up to Birmingham-Southern to enter the competition for their Phi Beta Kappa scholarship. The test was the usual multiple choice, fill-in-the-blank, and essay type of ordeal. I remember distinctly the essay topic I chose: "Write about a book that has had an influence on your life." I wrote a short essay about a biography of John Wesley, called *The Burning Thirst*. Birmingham-Southern was a Methodist school so I knew what I was doing. After the tests were assessed, I was asked to come into a large room and sit at the head of a long table lined with academics who grilled me for about an hour. I then waited outside with a friend from Andalusia who had driven up with me to take the test. Eventually, someone from the big room came out and told me I had won the scholarship.

Before deciding the amount of scholarship money to be handed out, Birmingham-Southern required that my parents fill out an exhaustive questionnaire about our family's finances, which was sent off to Princeton for evaluation. Alas, they seemed to think we were pretty well off, something we found hard to comprehend, and consequently only awarded me $600 a year, well below what Huntingdon was offering with all their scholarships.

I've mentioned financial considerations were a big factor. I think that issue, coupled with the fact that Birmingham was another ninety miles farther from home than Montgomery, led my parents to pressure me to go to Huntingdon. Did I mention I had no desire to major in music? However, since I had no overriding desire to major in anything in particular at that point, I agreed to go to Huntingdon.

Sidebar: once, when I was about five, my mother took Judy, Marcia, and me up to Canada by train to visit our grandparents and assorted aunts, uncles, and cousins. Getting there necessitated a lengthy stay in Chicago Union Station. Perhaps the term "Great Hall" alarmed my mother because, as we rode into the station, she produced a harness and leash, something I had never seen before, and put it on me. In her later recounting, she claimed I seemed to enjoy it, pulling her along as I barked my way through Chicago Union. She said it drew strange, amused, and sometimes understanding glances from other people managing children through the crowd, but honestly, I have never seen a child in such a contraption before or since. Perhaps it became against the law. The real leash did me no harm and probably saved me from dashing in the path of a locomotive.

Likewise, I suppose the figurative leashes they put on me were well-intentioned. But I often wonder if I had gone to Birmingham-Southern, which was less conventional, and if I had been allowed more exploration of what I wanted to be when I grew up, how different my life might have been.

I enrolled at Huntingdon and developed an intense dislike for the piano and an inability to make myself practice, which mightily threatened my collegiate career. I decided to switch to organ as my major instrument, having enjoyed my foray playing one on the USS *Antietam*. But even that was uninspiring for me until my teacher gave me a piece called "Le Banquet Céleste" by Olivier Messiaen, a contemporary composer. The piece was eerie and plodding and in my favorite key: minor. I was hooked and never looked back.

Four years later, I gave the first senior organ recital at Huntingdon College that consisted solely of twentieth-century music. My dad had gamely invited the members of his congregation and, as I walked out to start the performance, I was met with a meadow of periwinkle blue. It was actually a sea of perfectly permed and coiffed, blue-rinsed heads. The elderly ladies of my dad's flock had decided to support his child's big college moment and enjoy a musical soiree, expecting to be lulled by familiar works of Bach and Buxtehude. Instead, they were bombarded by the strident strains of Hindemith's "Organ Sonata No. 2" and the quieter "Es kommt ein Schiff geladen" by Ernst Pepping.

When it was over and the ladies were leaving, they struggled to say nice things about my recital. Many a blue head of hair looked to be standing on end. The main comment among the usual innocuous observations was "some of your pieces were very loud," something Hindemith would surely have taken as a compliment.

Back to the beginning of the four years. Here I was at a small liberal arts Methodist college in a south Alabama town. One of those pseudo-Gothic campuses with rolling flower-covered lawns. Everyone White and everyone middle class. It had been an all-girls school but now had a number of male students, occasionally ones who flunked out of somewhere more prestigious and whose parents were financially able to "persuade" the college to accept their boys.

I entered the flow of college life with gusto and developed a coterie of women who shared my liberal thoughts and my wish to be anything other than an ordinary student. One of our favorite adventures came about as a result of the college's financial officer, Deacon Reeves, deciding he would stop all walking on the grass by putting up a plethora of chains. We girls stayed up one night making miles of paper chains and numerous posters that said things like "Berlin has its walls; Huntingdon has its chains." We placed them all over the main building, Flowers Hall, and, using a real chain, padlocked the Deacon's office door shut. Everybody but the Deacon thought it was pretty funny, but even he managed to take it fairly gracefully and took down the chains. The incident prompted my history professor, Dr. Chappell, to say to me, "You know, Ellen, you're more interested in making history than learning it." Pretty perceptive fellow. I wasn't through yet.

On June 21, 1964, something happened that made my undertakings with the segregated Dairy Queen windows and

"Colored" drinking fountains seem trivial. Three civil rights workers disappeared in Philadelphia, Mississippi. Their bodies were found buried in an earthen dam six weeks later. It took a long time, but eventually eight members of the Ku Klux Klan went to prison on federal conspiracy charges; none served more than six years.

But I was doing my best. Always when I rode any bus— Brewton, Prattville, Montgomery—I marched to the back and sat down. Rosa Parks had supposedly made where you sat on a bus irrelevant. This good news hadn't filtered down to one particular bus driver in Montgomery. As always, I tromped to the back of the bus and settled down. From his driver's seat up front, he yelled back at me that I was sitting in the wrong place and to get up front. When I refused, he started yelling obscenities at me. It was making all the Black people on the bus very uncomfortable, so when he pulled the bus over and demanded I get out, I did. I recall it was on Sayres Avenue, a street named after Zelda Fitzgerald's family. Zelda probably would have exchanged vituperative word after vituperative word—but I was the well brought up preacher's daughter.

My junior year, in 1965, was rife with civil rights actions in Montgomery. The same gang of enlightened girls watched our school bunker down with signs posted everywhere that read, "Huntingdon College students are forbidden to appear at any areas of demonstration."

Now, *there* was a red flag for anyone interested in civil rights and what was happening before our very eyes. Here was history on our doorstep, as the United States of America moved inexorably toward what had begun with the Emancipation Proclamation in 1862. When the marchers were finally allowed to travel from Selma to Montgomery, there was no way this White girl—who drank from the fountains marked "Colored," who could never get served at that

Dairy Queen, and who walked home when she got kicked off the bus for sitting in the back— would miss being there to greet them.

The same seven girls who had hung those paper chains headed out to meet the marchers. I hoped no one would find out I had a scholarship from the Daughters of the Confederacy.

When we arrived at the field in front of the City of St. Jude hospital where the marchers were scheduled to arrive in the evening, we were astounded to find tens of thousands of people who had the same intentions. Only they were all Black and the seven of us girls stuck out as the only people who weren't. It was frightening and exhilarating all at the same time.

My roommate, Jeanne Bailey, and I got separated from the other girls and were immediately befriended by a group of Black kids, who asked who we were and why we were there. We got caught up in the power of the moment. Although deep down inside we knew we would never see these kids again, for a brief time, all seemed right with the world. When we noticed it was nearing our dormitory curfew and told them we had to leave, somehow the crowd miraculously fell back, leaving a pathway for us with everybody along the way thanking us for coming.

We floated back to the dorm where we hit the earth with a mighty thud when our house mother angrily accosted us, saying we were really "in for it" and had to appear before the dean of students, Charles Turner, at ten o'clock the next morning. It turned out that another dean, Mr. Owens, was a member of the National Guard and was on duty that night at St. Jude's. Evidently, we had walked right past him during our heartwarming exit from the field.

I went to bed and slept soundly. After all, how could a school official known as "The Silver Fox" do great harm to my friends and me? He had never even mentioned the chains escapade to me. Nor had he ever acknowledged that I might have had anything to do with the Huntingdon Chorus' version of Bach's "Mass in B minor," which included a section that sounded suspiciously like "clitoris peccata mundi."

So, we seven apprehended offenders arrived right on time the next day, full of confidence and, to be truly honest, self-righteousness.

Now, for the most remarkable part of the story. When the seven of us trudged over to the dean's office that morning, we found some twenty other students waiting for us outside the dean's door. They were the real heroes. They hadn't been caught, but they turned themselves in in support of us and were set to take whatever punishment ensued.

I agreed to be the spokesperson for us all. I walked into Mr. Turner's office and, before he had a chance to say a word, said, "You ought to fall down on your knees and thank God that you have students like us who choose to do what's right, not just what's popular. This college will inevitably have to accept Colored students, and you'll need enlightened and caring kids to ease the way." He sputtered about our deplorable behavior and threatened expulsion for us all.

The threat lessened to removing all our college offices from us until he realized that the heads of every major campus organization were in the group. More sputtering.

When all the dust settled, and the school had ultimately done nothing more punitive than post an innocuous statement on the bulletin boards—"We deplore the actions of those students who appeared in areas of demonstration"—we found we were never going to suffer anything worse than being shunned.

And shun they did. I don't know about the other girls because they were a year ahead of me, and I never noticed what happened in their scholastic lives except that they graduated with honors. But I know what happened to me. Though I also graduated with honors, my name mysteriously never appeared in *Who's Who in American Colleges and Universities,* though I had been told it would. Each year, a group of graduating students concocted a Last Will & Testament in which they left things to students coming up. In the 1966 version, they had me leaving my heart to Jasper, a young Black man who worked in the Huntingdon cafeteria. I imagine they thought that was very funny.

I had the pleasure of hearing snickering behind my back and having fellow students cross the hall to avoid the taint of association with me. But I wore the shunning proudly, presuming that it somehow gave me a very tiny bit of insight into the challenges faced daily by people of color.

I wasn't living in the world that Emmett Till had faced, but it was a setting that had the potential for danger. A childhood friend of mine, Martha Turnipseed, who went to Birmingham-Southern and had become more daring than I was, participated in a number of demonstrations such as sitting in with her Black friends at the Woolworth's lunch counter in Birmingham. The risk of placing oneself within immediate reach of irate White men took more courage than ordering a hot dog through the wrong window at the Dairy Queen. And her school, Birmingham-Southern, appeared to be less open-minded than Montgomery's Huntingdon College because hers booted her out, essentially putting her education on hold. She later sued them and won a settlement, which she immediately donated to the cause, and her subsequent career appeared no worse for the limbo in her formal education.

When Martha and I were little girls, we were quite theological, though Martha was always a deeper thinker than I was. I recall her once saying vehemently, "I wish Jesus would come down to earth and get a face and walk around."

Once during a childhood snack when I asked my mother where God was and was told he was everywhere, I observed, "Well, he's all over popcorn right now."

Mr. Rohlig

I DON'T KNOW IF an older adult rightfully belongs in these reminiscences, but I must include a man who had a permanent influence on my way of thinking. Maybe now that we are so much older, we would call each other Harald and Ellen, but back in the 1960s, he was always Mr. Rohlig.

You'll recall that I had inadvertently become a music major at Huntingdon College, and in an attempt to try to make it more palatable, switched from piano to organ. The palatable part was Harald Ernst Hermann Rohlig. Everything about him was different and interesting, starting with how he came to be sitting beside me on an organ bench in Montgomery, Alabama.

Born in Aurich, Germany in 1926, he was raised by a Methodist minister who instilled in his son beliefs and philosophies that would make him an inappropriate candidate for the German Air Force, which he was conscripted into in 1943. He told me that he purposefully set out to be captured by the Americans or the French. He was successful in this aim and spent three years in a French prison camp.

At one point in his internment, he was given the task of locating land mines. This resulted in an explosion that incapacitated one of his hands, but nothing was done to repair the damage.

Christmas came, and a prison camp guard polled the prisoners, looking for someone who could play Christmas carols. Harald volunteered. The guard laughed, pointing out his useless hand. No one else came forth, and they were forced to let the one-handed prisoner play, something he did so beautifully that the French officers called in a specialist to repair the damage.

He was released from the prison camp in 1948 and went back to his musical studies, which eventually took him to the Royal Academy of Music in London. When he finished with his schooling, he and his wife, Inge, a violinist, decided to immigrate to the United States. They were sponsored by a church in Linden, Alabama, and eventually moved their family to Montgomery.

Hence my good fortune in finding myself on that bench with a man who, as well as being an extremely gifted musician and teacher, was also a gifted storyteller and a man of astonishing integrity, all filtered through an engaging sense of humor and an appreciation of quirkiness. Through no fault of his, I never reached any remarkable heights as an organist, but I hung on his every word. From him, I learned orthodoxy, while at the same time learning to embrace liberalism even more vehemently. In those hours we spent on that bench, I learned how to let my mind and spirit soar.

When I asked him to fill out a form for me to enter graduate school, on the line marked "appearance" he wrote, "Delightfully tousled."

Years later, we talked at length at a college reunion. He asked me if I would accompany him as page-turner for a European organ performance tour. I was all set, but my husband at the time emphatically forbade me to go, and although I didn't cite it in my divorce application later, I did always hold that against him!

Hampstead

ON A MORE FRIVOLOUS note, let me tell you about life in a girls' dorm before the enlightened days of mixed housing and Wi-Fi in every room. Boys stayed outside, and girls stayed in. We played a lot of bridge and smoked countless cigarettes. Some of us occasionally even studied. We were prissy little White girls trying to be cool in a Methodist college dorm, that's for sure. Booze was cause for expulsion, though we drank our share of beer and Red Dagger wine when outside the campus confines and ate a lot of breath mints when it was time to return to our beds.

But one activity any self-respecting college girl engaged in was dating. One might think that, on a campus that had once been all-girls and where girls still outnumbered boys, there might have been slim pickin's. But then there were "town boys" and boys who showed up from students' hometowns or who were friends of friends. For some reason, we all felt compelled to persuade each other to go on "blind dates."

I was usually a bit leery about getting in a car with someone I didn't know but for only one degree of separation ("You've got to meet him; I've known him for years, and he's absolutely adorable . . .”). However, I occasionally let myself be persuaded.

One particular night, a classmate named Mary Anne Lanier talked me into going out with someone. I dutifully got dressed and waited in my room for the buzzer announcing the stranger's arrival. I bounced down the stairs, popped through the door, pointed to the guy, and chirpily said, "Blind date?" He equally chirpily replied, "Yep," and we scooted off into the night.

As we hopped into his Austin-Healey, top down, things were looking good. He was cute, his car was cute, and we were talking a mile a minute about politics (a dangerous topic when you didn't really know someone and all you wanted to say was, "Oh Lord, please don't let Goldwater win"), movies, current songs, and our current favorite academic subjects. Everything was fine until I called him Ira, and he asked, "Who's Ira?"

I replied, "Aren't you?"

He said, "My name's Hampstead Bentley. Everybody calls me Hampy."

Then he got a funny look on his face. "What's your name?"

"Ellen Nichols."

We both started laughing hysterically as it dawned on us: wrong blind date. Screech of wheels, quick U-turn, and a mad dash back to the dormitory, we rushed into the lobby where we found a very perplexed-looking couple. As we walked toward them, Hampy whispered, "I'll call you later," and we started to explain to the mystified couple what had happened. They didn't think it was as funny as we did, and the second go around with my real blind date wasn't nearly as much fun as the ten minutes with Hampy.

The next day, Hampy called. It turned out he lived in a perfect Southern situation with two maiden aunts who doted on him and did things like give him an Austin-Healey. He was Mr. Preppy, perfectly buttoned down and never seen without a tweedy sports jacket. He was très cool and I was mad about him. Funny, I was so mad about him that all these years later, I can't remember what happened to us. Who broke up with whom? Or who moved away? I just remember I liked him a lot and we always had fun. Shoot, how could bombing around in a Healey with the top down be anything *but* fun?

Robert

ROBERT HAD A TRIUMPH. It was a robin's egg–blue convertible with right-hand drive. He was British, you know, and so doesn't rightly belong in a saga filled with Southern boys and men, but he was a wannabe Southern man—at least at first.

In my junior year, I belonged to the International Relations Club and went to all the meetings because the speakers were usually people from far-off places and thus more interesting than those in the immediate surroundings. A speaker at one Club event was a young Englishman, who was taking a year off after receiving his doctor of philosophy in history from Oxford and before he headed into the Foreign Service. James Bond on my doorstep.

He spoke eloquently of relations between England, Canada, and the US, all in a divine British accent, so I hung on every word. During his talk, he referred to Arthur Meighen, a prime minister in Canada during the 1920s. One of my Canadian uncles, Roger Graham, had written a three-volume definitive biography of Meighen, so of course I had to twirl up after his speech and discuss said prime minister and tell him about my uncle. We talked about the amazing coincidence and decided to go for a cup of coffee. He hadn't really explained to the group how he came to be in Montgomery of all places, so I was eager to find that out; plus, it meant I could listen to the charming accent a bit longer.

Oh Lord, when I heard he had come to the US to teach at the Montgomery Academy for a year, I thought the relationship would have to end right there. The school was one of those independent grammar/high schools that sprang up in the 1960s so that the children of wealthy racists wouldn't have to go to school with classmates of color. These schools usually had the word "Academy" in their names, and most often the word Christian appeared too. The travesty that this practice wreaked on the educational system of Alabama played a part in the many years that the state languished at the bottom of the rankings, with only Mississippi below, whenever an assessment of the quality of American schools was made.

But as I got to know Robert, I realized what a joke had been played on the Montgomery Academy. His unsuspecting British cousin, transplanted to the wilds of south Alabama, had plunked the very liberal, highly educated Robert down in the midst of a bunch of children whose parents thought they were insulating their precious White children from any trace of the "tarbrush" and any danger of learning to think independently and originally. Their children had the advantage of being taught by an enlightened mind and soul, bent on instilling rational thinking skills into their stifled little brains. And probably no one even realized it, otherwise the British gentleman would have been ousted posthaste, and I would never have had the privilege of knowing him.

We dated for a whole year. In fact, he came back for a second year, partly because the post he sought in England wasn't yet available to him, but also because of his professed fondness for the Methodist preacher's daughter who, along with her family members, showed him that not all Alabama dwellers were slack-jawed, racist yokels.

Now, here comes one of the great mistakes of my life. I didn't accept his proposal to spend the rest of my life with him and, like a fool, sent him on his way without me. I have always regretted that.

Years later, when my mother died and I was going through her address book, writing to anyone who might not hear of her passing, I discovered an address for Robert Griffiths at Ripon, North Yorkshire, England. She had kept in touch with him all those years! I wrote to him that she was gone and that I was amazed the two of them had kept in touch.

He wrote back a letter that overwhelmed me with his enthusiasm at the prospect of seeing each other again, which in turn called forth an equally ebullient letter from me. Letters, growing more torrid with each posting, sailed back and forth. I let a good friend in on the secret of the reviving romance, and she agreed to let him send his letters to her address. I was married to my second Canadian husband at the time, and never has a more suspicious person existed. He grilled me about the origin of every bruise that ever appeared on my body during our marriage. So, you can see my cause for trepidation, titillating though the whole adventure was.

I composed my letters to Robert on an early edition computer and didn't quite have the knack of hiding them well. Also, I couldn't bear not to keep his letters and read them constantly, so I hid them at my own home—alas, not well enough. The cuckolded-by-mail husband found my letters on the computer, then proceeded to ransack the house until he found the ones I had received from Robert. He confronted me and literally forced me to call England to say it was over while he stood by, an ending that lasted just long enough for me to get out of the house alone and find a phone.

Funny, when we got a divorce, my husband said he had saved the letters I wrote because they were so beautifully written. He said it made him sad because I had never written anything like that to him.

And what was the denouement of this tale, you ask? That will have to wait for the saga of the second half of my life.

Skippy

SUICIDE SEEMS TO BE a bit of a theme in my beaus' lives—fortunately theirs, not mine. I've never felt any desire to shuffle off this mortal coil, and I like to think I didn't contribute to anybody else's desire to do so, but who ever knows about these things. The people one might question are no longer talking.

I knew Skippy in college. He was actually the son of the president of Huntingdon College. He wasn't a student but was still living at home and hanging around the campus. I can't remember how I met him, just that I was mesmerized by his piercing pale blue eyes. He was a good-looking fellow with an infectious grin that came over his face real slow. And he liked me.

It was the time of Bob Dylan, calico dresses, hair down to my waist, and soul searching. Skippy did a lot of soul searching. I should have had a premonition when I learned that his favorite song was "See That My Grave Is Kept Clean," but I didn't. We were all caught up in wondering who we were and why we were put on this earth: typical college junior thoughts. Life was exciting, times were a-changin', and death was far away.

When I first met Skippy, he was in the throes of trying to figure out what to do about having gotten his girlfriend pregnant. In a nearby town (the one Virgil hailed from), I had an uncle who was a doctor with his own clinic. I had previously had an interesting experience with one of my uncle's partners, who had tried to get me to meet him for a drink and hinted that we would share more than a martini. I turned him down, but I had an inkling that perhaps this particular doctor might be amenable to helping remedy Skippy's unfortunate situation. I sent him and his hapless ex-girlfriend over to see him.

As it turned out, the girlfriend's father found out and had his own doctor, so the problem was solved. But of course, the young lady was no longer allowed to see the president's son and that's how I got involved. The new girl. No danger of my getting pregnant. I was still heavily into being a preacher's daughter and heavily into saving others from perdition. But I sure didn't save him.

As we got to know each other, Skippy unraveled a tale of a misspent childhood and youth, which ended when he entered the Navy (the childhood and youth part, not the misspent aspect). I think he was stationed in Korea, but it might have been Japan. When I queried why he was no longer in uniform but back in his dad's house, he told me a story that sounded bizarre but which I later found out was true. He had been responsible for the death of a fellow serviceman, said death having taken place in a bar. Skippy said he couldn't remember why and offered no details as to what actually took place. He never served hard time for it, unless you call time at Bryce Mental Hospital in Tuscaloosa hard time.

Now, wouldn't you think I would say, "Whoa, let me out of this!" as soon as this story started to unfold? But no, like a moth to the flame, I loved it. The relationship puttered along, with me trying to redeem this drifting soul, until one steamy night in the college parking lot. They would call it attempted date rape now, but I just called it scary. I decided this was more excitement than I had bargained for and begged off the relationship. By some miracle, he let me go peacefully, if tearfully.

Several years later, I heard he died by his own hand. I hope he's buried in one of those perpetual care cemeteries that will see that his grave is kept clean.

Aubrey

I'M GOING TO SIDETRACK a bit from the suicide motif. However, I suppose you could fit Aubrey in here nicely because he had attempted the act several times. By last count, he hadn't succeeded, though he seemed to be in the midst of a long, slow attempt via alcohol and pills. I always thought of him as a Dylanesque (Thomas, not Bob) type of character: just off-center and seemingly bent on self-destruction.

Now, Aubrey I really liked. He was one of the most intelligent, well-read, learned people I've ever spent time with—one of those people who make you breathless just trying to keep up with his thoughts. He was a person who made you want to read frantically, think constantly, and thirst for knowledge. I loved that in a setting where most of the young men around me were playing bridge or worried about the college's basketball standing. I loved Aubrey for making me think, but Lord, he was an unbalanced man.

He was enrolled in an ongoing summer treatment program at Johns Hopkins Hospital after having spent several years there as a full-time patient. His diagnosis: paranoid schizophrenia. Many times, he told me about the voices that talked to him, and many times I saw an innocent remark of mine twisted into an unrecognizable threatening assault in his mind.

One night at the end of a date, we parked in a grammar school yard near the college. Remember back when students spent so much time in parking lots? It's a wonder we didn't all suffer from some impairment of the limbs due to contortions under the steering wheel. Thank God coed dorms arrived just in time to save students from the agony of bucket seats. Anyway, Aubrey and I had been contorting for some time when he suddenly sat up and began to furiously berate me for trying to make him feel guilty. After all, I had suggested that we stop in this church parking lot. Obviously I had done this on purpose because my father was a minister. Whew! It didn't matter that I pointed out it was a school (glad he didn't know my mother was a teacher). He was sure it was a church and became almost violent.

I managed to make it back to the dorm in one piece, but that was the end of Aubrey and me. We still had German class together, but he usually arrived drunk and so didn't even notice me. I recall his taking the final exam while totally inebriated and getting one hundred percent on it. Told you he was smart.

Dickie

ANOTHER EXAMPLE OF MY propensity for not latching onto the right guy was Dickie Calhoun. He was studying to be a lawyer, was very attractive, ambitious, had good sense, and—what could be more perfect?—was the son of a Methodist minister. So, of course, the romance couldn't possibly last.

He was in law school at the University of Alabama, so we trekked back and forth from Montgomery to Tuscaloosa. My favorite memory was going to see him for Law Weekend, during which we managed to stay awake and party for forty-eight straight hours. Never mind I had to be back in Montgomery by noon on Sunday to participate in the annual May Day festivities. I looked stultified in all the subsequent photos of the event. But it was worth it.

This was in the mid-1960s and, when we weren't scrambling from party to party, we sat on the porch of the house he shared with what seemed like a dozen other law students. Music was always playing, and the beer was always cold. Nobody had a care in the world until somebody ran out on the porch and yelled, "Dylan's just announced he's going electric!"

Sure, I remember where I was when Kennedy died, but just as clearly, I remember when Dylan slid off that hippy-dippy, anthem-singing acoustic course and became electrified. We all thought he was making a serious mistake!

But we still had our favorite non-electric band, Hank and the Red Lighters, a quasi-Ike & Tina Turner group. When Hank et al. didn't come into town, we went to them, which was always exciting and a bit scary all at the same time. It involved a trip to the country and entering a poorly lit, ramshackle, nightclub kind of a place. The air seemed electric to us as we meandered in.

But the music. The music! Never have I felt so free on a dance floor. This one was almost slippery with sweat, including mine. I felt as if the music took over my limbs and sent them in directions I would never have been able to dream up on my own, never mind execute. I proved that I was a *Soul Train* girl, not a namby-pamby *American Bandstand* girl. No bright lights for me—bring on the torch songs.

Nobody was ever anything but welcoming, but just in case, Dickie made me swear that if anyone asked me to dance, I was to do so. Funny, nobody ever did. They were probably having too much fun watching the White kids try to be as cool as they were and not succeeding.

Chip

THE ONLY TIME IN my life I was ever "pinned" was when I wore Chip Letton's Vanderbilt Sigma Chi fraternity pin. In fact, it was the "pinning" that was the undoing of our inchoate relationship.

Chip and his father lived in a little house at the northeast end of the Huntingdon College campus. I can't remember what his dad had to do with the college, but they lived on the grounds.

When I met Chip, he had just received his Bachelor of Engineering (magna cum laude) from Vanderbilt University, was working on his MS, and later headed to Georgia Tech for a PhD in electrical engineering. His subsequent career included manufacturing and research in multiphase flow measurement, wet gas flow measurement, ultrasonic flow meters, optical flow meters, and digital signal processing.

I know, I know. About now you're wondering how he managed to communicate with this music major. He managed because he was truly a nice guy without a snobby bone in his body. Also, he became a Navy man for some years, and you already know about my penchant for Navy guys. He actually went on to be a Navy engineer/ engineering manager and led a project team that developed the

Navy's first ship-to-ship laser communication system. I could have used his expertise when I was attempting to play that wheezy little organ on the USS *Antietam*.

Chip had made good against many odds. His mother had died when he was very young, and he and his dad had to fend for themselves in an era when women were most often the ones who turned a house into a home. A mother usually did the important cooking, kept the house clean and in order, made sure you were properly and warmly dressed, and that you did your homework. Somehow, when you visited Chip and his dad in their house, there was a poignant feeling in the air of two lost guys trying to make it appear that all was just fine in their home, but not quite pulling it off.

Chip had this attention-arresting scar on his right forearm. I, being the polite soul I was, didn't ask him about its origin. One night, we snuck a swim in the Montgomery Country Club pool just across the street from his house, the very same pool that Zelda and F. Scott used to jump into in full fancy dress attire. Only we had on no attire and were skinny-dipping very quietly around the darkened pool in titillating fear that, at any moment, glaring lights would reveal us, a small siren would sound, the Club caretaker would descend on us, and we would have a lot of explaining to do.

That was the time Chip chose to tell me about the scar that gleamed in the moonlight with every stroke of his arm. He and a friend had been driving in the friend's car when a truck ran a red light and plowed into them at full speed. The friend didn't survive and, though the friend had been driving, Chip always felt guilty that he had walked away from the wreck relatively intact. The injury to his arm was nothing compared to the injury the tragedy had on his mind: first, devastation at the loss of his friend and then the post-traumatic nightmares, and a lasting feeling of "if only."

Once we had established our Montgomery relationship, nothing would do but that I go to visit him on his academic turf. Neither one of us had any money to speak of, so I set out from Montgomery to Nashville in the intrepid Clyde. Obviously, I was in love enough to risk going beyond the Montgomery city limits in a vehicle that was only allowed on the road because they didn't have those pesky road-worthiness requirements back then.

Nashville is known as the "Athens of the South" because of its many colleges and universities, most notable of which is Vanderbilt. It actually has a replica of the Parthenon, and of course there's the Hermitage, the home of Andrew Jackson, aka "Old Hickory," one of the most authentically preserved homes of a US president. Chip made sure I saw the best that Nashville had to offer.

And "the best" included heart-stoppingly romantic moments in his cozy student apartment, moments that culminated in his "pinning" me with his Sigma Chi pin—the first step toward becoming engaged and the first step toward the unraveling of our romance.

In modern-day parlance, I would probably be dubbed "commitment-phobic." Indeed, I never was one of those girls who spent my teenage years planning my future wedding. I never had a stack of *Brides* magazines piled up around my dorm room. I never thought about who I would ask to be my bridesmaids, or what we would all wear. I never planned what processional music would be played.

I just never was very good at being that traditional Southern belle, and I wasn't mature enough to realize the dangers of falling headlong into the hippie abyss.

Unfortunately for Chip, and unfortunately for me.

Steve

HIS FINGERNAILS WERE LONGER than mine, and I loved him probably because my mother never would have. He was a folk singer and one amazing guitar player. And he was the kind of guy who later named his son Jubal Lee.

He came from a town smaller than any I had ever lived in—Gadsden, Alabama. His daddy drove the only taxi in town, an old Checker cab like the ones that used to be in New York, and was always so inebriated that passengers often had their trips across town interrupted while Mr. Young stopped to throw up beside the cab. I fear large tips were not a part of the Young family income.

However, Steve was extremely talented musically and made his way to California in the 1960s. He was a guitar session player for the Kingston Trio and other groups. I remember being shocked to find out that all that fancy pickin' on their albums wasn't done by them. He also played on an album with two friends from Gadsden, Richard Lockmiller and Jim Connor. It was recorded with Capitol Records, *Folk Songs and Country Sounds,* and I still have a copy of it. Richard Fariña had written the jacket notes, which rambled on about small-town boys making their way to California, all that

1960s stuff about traveling on down the highway. Fariña only mentioned Steve's name in passing even though, again, he was the one on the album doing all the fancy pickin'.

When you listen to it all these years later, you still have to marvel at his playing. I can't remember why he turned up in Montgomery in early 1966, but a mutual friend, Jimmy Evans, introduced us. Steve was outlandish by Montgomery standards—long hair, cowboy boots, and the aforementioned long fingernails, at least on his right hand—and I loved him instantly. I had straight hair down to my waist, affected long flour-sack dresses and sandals, and was majoring in music, albeit Bach and Buxtehude, at that stronghold of Methodism, Huntingdon College. It was the year after I had almost been kicked out of school for going down to welcome the Selma marchers. He seemed to fall in love with me too. I guess he looked past the preacher's daughter persona and saw me for the true folkie dopie I was.

Our first date was on a Sunday afternoon, and I had to be at church at 6:30 p.m. for some kind of Methodist youth happening. As we drove up to the church, I went all limp and fell out of sight on the car seat, protesting that I really didn't want to go. I remember he found that funny. I did go, though, because my daddy was the preacher at that church and expected me to be there. Fortunately, or maybe unfortunately in some opinions, I stayed in the college dormitory instead of at home, or I never would have had the adventures I had.

Steve was my first advanced sexual experience as, so far, I had never gotten past the look-and-fondle stage. I realize in hindsight that I was truly living on the edge. Birth control pills weren't readily available yet. I certainly couldn't go to the family doctor for a diaphragm. In fact, I don't recall I even knew what a diaphragm was.

I guess his not being into frequent sex that much helped. It's only upon looking back that I realize why. I estimate he was thoroughly stoned ninety percent of the time. We never talked about drugs, and I had no experience with anything beyond the surreptitious beer so dear to Huntingdon students. I say surreptitious because it was a teetotal school in the true Methodist tradition, and alcohol consumption was a matter for expulsion. So, with no frame of reference, I presumed he was just naturally a bit foggy. And as for the level of interest in sex usually found in men in their twenties, I had no frame of reference for that either.

I was intrigued and titillated by a two-foot-long scar which wrapped around his chest and back. When I asked the natural question about how it happened, he was very evasive. I never did get a real answer, except that he had been shot during his teenage, Gadsden days. The way he always described his hometown, laid back and lethargic, it was hard to imagine someone being shot there.

I once went back to Gadsden with him to a family reunion of the Horselys. They were his mother's folks, kind, gentle, and interesting, and they took me right in. The food was incredible and kept with the Southern tradition of a table with no empty space on it: fried chicken, country-fried steak, pork chops, mashed potatoes, home fries, scalloped potatoes, pole beans, green beans, crowder peas, okra, bean salad, two types of potato salad, and big fluffy green salad all washed down with jugs of sweet tea and topped off with melt-in-your-mouth banana pudding and hand-churned ice cream.

There was much sitting on the porch and listening to stories told by master raconteurs who recounted tales of who had the best stills, whose husbands had slept with whose wives, and who had won the prize for the biggest turnip. I couldn't get enough.

I hated to leave, but Steve couldn't wait to get out of there. There was no appearance of his father and no mention of him other than the recounting of the taxi escapades. I think maybe he was dead.

Steve, Jimmy Evans, and I were a constant trio. Jimmy had a car and, unless I borrowed my dad's, we were dependent on Jimmy's to get us around. The Montgomery transit system was okay, but as mentioned before, I had once been thrown off one of their buses for sitting at the back, and I was a bit fearful of getting the same quasi-violent driver again. So, we went everywhere with Jimmy. Looking back, I'm not sure why he never had a date; he was certainly the best looking of us three, but he was often around and always on his own.

Though the Selma march had been some months before, those were still the days of Bull Connor, Al Lingo, and "Stand in Your Doorway" George Wallace. An Alabama gubernatorial race was pending. George couldn't succeed himself, so his wife Lurleen ran instead. Never mind that she was suffering from cancer, and indeed died in office. Her chief rival was Attorney General Richmond Flowers, who, likely realizing there was no way in Hell to compete with the Wallace machine, campaigned on a civil rights platform. Maybe he really believed in the cause of integration. I was never sure. But I knew I did.

We joined in the gubernatorial campaign and worked hard for Flowers in hopes of defeating Lurleen. We wore buttons that said, "I'm too old for a governess." We stumped into the Black churches and sang "The Lonesome Death of Hattie Carroll" until we were hoarse. But we were always singing to the converted, and there weren't enough of them, or at least not enough who had been allowed to register to vote. Lurleen won.

Later, Richmond Flowers was convicted of some kind of fraud and shipped off to the state penitentiary. We all just knew he had been framed, and indeed in later years there was a campaign to exonerate him. After the election, we kept company with Bill Baxley who later became attorney general of Alabama and led the fight to bring the Birmingham Sunday bombers to justice. Those were heady days.

Once Jimmy, Steve, and I went to New Orleans for the weekend back when it was safe and you could wander from club to club all night—which we did. We stayed with a friend, Kenny Austin. I recall he was a lawyer and played one hell of a banjo. Both nights, after we finished our tour of the clubs, we went back to Kenny's house on Toulouse Street, where he and Steve would play the rest of the night. I especially remember their romping version of "Salty Dog." I was transported because I had never been so close to living musicians who could play like that.

Just as dawn was breaking on the warm Sunday morning, it started to rain. I wandered out into the courtyard reveling in the dampness. I could hear them playing through the window. Somehow, clothes seemed inappropriate, so I took them off one by one, leaving a trail along the wet grass, and danced naked in the courtyard. At one point, I looked up and saw a man in another house on the courtyard, watching me from his window. Our eyes locked and I kept on dancing. It was eerie and enchanted, and I remember it vividly all these years later.

We reluctantly left the next day, just in time for the sunset as we rode across that long bridge outside New Orleans. The sun was behind us as we headed east, but the entire sky was colored red like some Mephistophelean vision. We rode through the night with the windows down. It was steamy and the seams of the highway were twanging. I never wanted it to end.

Steve wrote a song for me about the enchantment of the whole experience and about letting me out in the town where I was born. It all still seems so real.

He wrote another song about the road in Montgomery, where we used to park and make out when I borrowed my daddy's car and before Steve had an apartment. It was called Woodley Road, but everyone referred to it as "Seven Bridges Road." The Eagles made it famous. But I remember the way it sounded when he wrote it, and I was the one who heard it first. I wrote out the notes for him on music notation paper. As he did in that song, Steve was always singing and writing songs about leaving. But I was the one who moved on down the highway first.

There was an element of siren singing to that whole relationship. But before I hit the rocks, I left to attend graduate school in Toronto, Canada. He couldn't understand why I was going and was really hurt and angry about it. But I had made the plans long before and, because I naively thought our love would last forever, I went. We wrote beautiful letters and had long, passionate phone calls, even after he went back to California. But the distance between Los Angeles and Toronto took its toll and eventually we lost touch. Until some years later.

I had been married, divorced, and was living on my own with my young son in Canada. I had a dignified job as supervisor of the therapeutic recreation program at the Hospital for Sick Children. The flour sack dresses were gone and the long hair was most often wound up in a French twist. I dressed a bit more sedately but did introduce culottes to my wardrobe (those combo pants/skirts jumpers) as the perfect garment to wear when working with kids. My 1960s soul was still intact, but I was trying to behave like a grownup.

Well-meaning friends were always trying to fix me up, but I wasn't that fond of blind dates. So, when a couple I knew only slightly told me about their friend from Atlanta who came often to Toronto on business and was just perfect for me, I was reluctant. They kept at me and finally persuaded me to go out to dinner with the three of them.

During the dinner conversation, the visitor referred several times to his roommate, M. D. I don't know what prompted me but finally I asked, "By any chance is your roommate M. D. Garmon from Gadsden, Alabama? My boyfriend in college, Steve Young, was from Gadsden, and his best friend was named M. D."

We were never able to go back to that restaurant again. The shrieks of "I don't believe it" resounded. We all ran out of the restaurant and back to my house where we called M. D., who did his own shrieking. It was a bit scary. That couple picked me out of a city of some two million plus people. What were the chances?

M. D. immediately called his old Gadsden buddy, Steve, who became obsessed with the thought that this was some kind of karmic connection. And I guess it was. He flew up to Toronto, all set to live out some fated fantasy. Only, once he got to Toronto, we had nothing much to say to each other.

He was still in the same boots and cowboy hat, but I was different. We made half-hearted attempts to have sex, but it became painfully obvious that each of us couldn't wait to be out of the presence of the other. I guess what was missing was the stoned stupor on his part, as he obviously couldn't bring anything mood-enhancing across the border, especially looking like he did. As for little Miss Priss, I didn't have any such substances on hand and no idea where to get them. And since I was no longer caught up in the romance of the hippie madness of 1966, we had to putter along with little embellishment to each other's company.

Or maybe it was just that Thomas Wolfe was right: You can't go home again.

The New Land

LEAVING WAS IMPORTANT FOR a girl who just didn't fit the mold of the South's strict rules of behavior, especially the rules for women. Perhaps I should have stayed and kept trying to change things. I could have traded my civil rights temerity for women's rights.

But there was the call of a bigger place, so I left the categorical imperatives of the small-town south Alabama Methodist milieu for the heretical imperatives of big city life as I headed off to graduate school at the University of Toronto. Little did I know Toronto's nickname was "Hogtown," and that in the 1960s it was little more than a glorified small town. It didn't matter though because I thought I'd be there one year and then move to some glamorous American city.

Forty years later, I'm writing this book about the South from the vantage point of the frozen North with no regrets, except maybe about the frozen part. And yes, I did manage to find attractive, interesting, and unsuitable Canadian men, and even married a few of them—but that's for another book.

Acknowledgments

I WOULD LIKE TO thank the people who played a key role in this book happening:

John Pearce, who works for Westwood Creative Artists in Toronto. He and I served together on the board of Toronto's Esprit Orchestra and he offered to read my first manuscript. He praised it highly and encouraged me to expand it.

And then there is my son, Graham Sanders, who teaches courses at University of Toronto on literary Chinese and poetry of the Tang dynasty. He is a published author himself and edited my book beautifully. And a warm thank-you to his daughter, Mia, who designed a beautiful website for her grandmother at https://ellennichols.com.

The final editor was Courtney Meunier through Koehler Books Publishing. She polished my words even further and made me proud when she said reading my book was addictive.

I owe a huge debt to the accomplished author Cassandra King Conroy, for her time, talent, knowledge, and her spirit. She led me to Koehler Books Publishing, where John Koehler and Greg Fields embraced me (by Zoom, of course) and signed me up. And I am grateful to Koehler Books designer Kellie Emery for her gifted cover and interior-design sense. She and Joe Coccaro made me look good. And a big thank you to Tyler Smiley who made sure I had a tip sheet and book copies when needed.

And I am grateful to those with whom I worked over the years during my sojourn in Toronto and who loved my stories about growing up in the Deep South so much I decided to write them all down.

I owe a fond tribute to the late Elaine Mitchell, who facilitated the Toronto women writers' group I have belonged to for many years. She encouraged me to pursue publishing my memoir and offered many helpful suggestions.

Then there is my dear and faithful friend Elwood Saracuse, who read parts of it as I wrote it, and told me to stop buying lottery tickets and finish my book because he thought I had a much higher chance of finding fortune if I did that.

My former husband, Billy Sharma, of Designers Inc. Toronto, who always supported my writing and whose design sense heightened my success as a fundraiser over the years.

Many thanks to my friend David Snyder who helped me find an excellent publicist.

And last but not least. A huge thank-you to my current husband, Mike Ward, who when he first read my book told me, "One is captured with your openness, drawn deeply into the dialogue so much as to sometimes feel guilty of spying." And he will be the one supporting me through the excitement of book signings and promotional events.

The authenticity of this book comes directly from my memory of my life. If I seem harsh in remembering someone's actions, e.g., racist remarks, they wrote those words themselves, in offering such rhetoric in my presence. The same goes for praise. I wrote what I heard and what I observed.

CPSIA information can be obtained
at www.ICGtesting.com
Printed in the USA
LVHW102002120422
716026LV00017B/373/J